Mysticism in English Literature

Mysticism in English Literature

M.L. Shah

SWASTIK

SWASTIK PUBLICATIONS
DELHI - 110 094 (INDIA)

MYSTICISM IN ENGLISH LITERATURE

First Published 2011

ISBN 978-93-80138-90-9

Published in India by

SWASTIK PUBLICATIONS
31, Gali No. 1, A-Block, Pocket-5,
CRP Water Tank, Sonia Vihar
Delhi-110094 (INDIA)
email: swastik_books@yahoo.com

Printed at: Deepak Offset Press, Delhi.

Contents

Preface

"If the doors of perception were cleansed,
everything would appear to man as it is, infinite.
For man has closed himself up.
Till he sees all things through the narrow chinks of his cavern."

—*William Blake*

In common parlance, Mysticism is the pursuit of communion with, identity with, or conscious awareness of an ultimate reality, divinity, spiritual truth, or God through direct experience, intuition, instinct or insight.

Mysticism usually centers on a practice or practices intended to nurture those experiences or awareness. Mysticism may be dualistic, maintaining a distinction between the self and the divine, or may be nondualistic.

The present book is an endeavour to address and evaluate Mysticism and mystic literature in English. Though a philosophic and religious term at core, Mysticism has greatly influenced the world literature. Mysticism in diverse forms in different literary genres in English has been elaborately dealt with in this book. The vital information is gathered under the following chapter: What is Mysticism?; Origin and Development; Medieval Mysticism; Western Mysticism: An Overview; Nature Mystics and Mysticism; 20th Century Nature Mysticism; Love and Beauty Mystics; Philosophical Mysticism; The Mysticism of John Muir; Metaphysics and Metaphysical Poetry; John Donne; Conclusion; Bibliography and Glossary etc.

Students, researchers and teachers of English literature will find this informative and useful.

While working a this book, I have heavily drawn upon many standard works, penned by celebrated authors in the field. It is not possible to acknowledge them individually. All those names appear in Bibliography. I am deeply beholden to them for subscribing their views as well as works. I am sincerely grateful to my teachers, colleagues and friends for their encouragement, guidance and assistance. Last but not the least, I am grateful to my publishers for making this work available in the present shape.

Suggestions and comments from learned readers are welcome which may definitely enhance and improve the quality of information contained in this book.

—M.L. Shah

1

What is Mysticism?

> "Hence the saying: If you know the enemy and know yourself, you need not fear the result of a hundred battles. If you know yourself but not the enemy, for every victory gained you will also suffer a defeat. If you know neither the enemy nor yourself, you will succumb in every battle."
>
> —*Sun Tzu, The Art of War*

Since in the present book we intend to elucidate the mysticism in English literature, it is necessary to have a thorough understanding of Mysticism—the concept and meaning, theories, application and the goal.

Here in this chapter we shall introduce you to the Mysticism in pros and cons.

In common parlance, Mysticism is the pursuit of communion with, identity with, or conscious awareness of an ultimate reality, divinity, spiritual truth, or God through direct experience, intuition, instinct or insight.

Mysticism usually centers on a practice or practices intended to nurture those experiences or awareness. Mysticism may be dualistic, maintaining a distinction between the self and the divine, or may be nondualistic.

- Self-nullification (making oneself *bittel*, known as abnegation of the ego) and focus upon and absorption within Ein Sof Ohr: God's Infinite Light (Hassidic schools of Judaism)
- Complete non-identification with the world (Kaivalya in some schools of Hinduism, including Sankhya and Yoga; Jhana in Buddhism)
- Liberation from the cycles of Karma (Moksha in Jainism, Sikhism and Hinduism, Nirvana in Buddhism)
- Deep intrinsic connection to ultimate reality (Satori in Mahayana Buddhism, Te in Taoism)
- Union with God (Henosis in Neoplatonism and Brahma-Prapti or Brahma-Nirvana in Hinduism, *fana* in Sufism, mukti in Sikhism)
- Theosis or Divinization, union with God and a participation of the Divine Nature (in Catholic Christianity and Eastern Orthodoxy)
- Innate Knowledge (Sahaja and Svabhava in Hinduism; Irfan and Sufism in Islam)
- Experience of one's true blissful nature (Samadhi Svarupa-Avirbhava in Hinduism and Buddhism)
- Seeing the Light, or "that of God", in everyone (Hinduism, Quakerism, Sikhism)
- The Love of God, as in the Hinduism, Baha'i Faith, Christianity, Islam, Sikhism and many other spiritual traditions

It is pertinent to note that Mystic traditions form sub-currents within larger religious traditions—such as Kabbalah within Judaism, Sufism within Islam, Vedanta and Kashmir Shaivism within Hinduism, Christian mysticism (and arguably Gnosticism) within Christianity—but are often treated skeptically and sometimes held separately, by more orthodox or mainstream groups within the given religion, due to the emphasis of the mystics on direct experience and living realization over doctrine. Mysticism is sometimes taken by skeptics or mainstream adherents as mere obfuscation, though mystics suggest they are offering clarity of a different order or kind.

In fact, a basic premise of nearly every mystical path, regardless of religious affiliation, is that the experiences of divine consciousness, enlightenment and union with God that are made possible via mystical paths, are available to everyone who is willing to follow the practice of a given mystical system. Within a given mystical school, or path, it is much more likely for the mystical approach to be seen as a divine science, because of the direct, replicable elevation of consciousness the mystical approach can offer to anyone, regardless of previous spiritual or religious training. Some mystic traditions can exclude the validity of other traditions.

However, mystic traditions tend to be more accepting of other mystic traditions than the non-mystical versions of their traditions. This is based on the premise that the experienced divinity is able to bring other mystics to their own tradition if necessary.

It is foremost to mention that Underhill (1875–1941) published her seminal work (1911) foregrounding the focus of mysticism scholarship as praxis and from the experience of praxis or 'practice' rather than mere theory. Otto (1869–1937) in his Haskell Lectures at Oberlin College in 1924 presented his reprise on the consonance and divergence of mystical forms in their Eastern and Western evocations through his research into the case studies and types presented by Adi Shankara (788 CE - 820 CE) representing East, and Eckhart (c. 1260–c. 1328), the West. This suite of lectures was further expanded by Otto and published in a master work in German soon after and subsequently rendered into English by Bracy & Payne (1932).

In common parlance, '"Mysticism"' refers to beliefs and practices that go beyond the liturgical and devotional forms of worship of mainstream faith, often by seeking out inner or esoteric meanings of conventional religious doctrine, and by engaging in spiritual practices such as breathing practices, prayer, contemplation and meditation, along with chanting and other activities designed to heighten spiritual awareness. For example, Kabbalah (based in Judaism) seeks out deeper interpretations of the Torah and other mystical works, and may conduct spiritual practices based in Meditation, Theurgy, or Alchemy, as well as song, dance, prayer, and talmudic study, accordingly, as is done in many other mystical traditions. Sufism (in Islam) extends and amplifies the teachings of the Quran in the spirit of universal love, most famously through their devotional musicians dancing Zhikrs and singing Qawwalis.

Vedanta reaches for the inner teachings of Hindu philosophy encapsulated in the Vedas, and many students of both Shaivite Tantric schools within Hinduism, as well as Shakta Tantrics, along with usually more mainstream-oriented Vaisnaivas, will use the symbolism and mythologies of their gods and goddessess, to take the initiate home to their highest awareness, via mystical practices designed and proven for these purposes. Mystics hold that there is a deeper or more fundamental state of existence beneath the observable, day-to day world of phenomena, and that in fact the ordinary world is superficial or epiphenomenal.

Often mysticisms center on the teachings of individuals who are considered to have special insight, and in some cases entire non-mystical (doctrine-based) faiths have arisen around these leaders and their teachings, with few or no mystical practitioners remaining. Different faiths have differing relationships to mystical thought. Hinduism has many mystical sects, in part due to its historic reliance on gurus (individual teachers of insight) for transmission of its philosophy. Mysticism in Buddhism is largely monastic, since most Buddhists consider jhana (meditation) to be an advanced technique used only after many lifetimes.

Mysticism in Abrahamic religions is largely marginalized, from the tolerance mainstream Muslims grant to Sufism to the active fears of cultism prevalent among western Christians, with Chasidic Kabbalists of Judaism being the notable exceptions.

Mysticisms generally hold to some form of immanence, since their focus on direct realization obviates many concerns about the afterlife, and this often conflicts with conventional religious doctrines. Mystical teachings are passed down through transmission from teacher to student, though the relationship between student and teacher varies: some groups require strict obedience to a teacher, others carefully guard teachings until students are deemed to be ready, in others a teacher is merely a guide aiding the student in the process.

It is significant to note that Mysticism may make use of canonical and non-canonical religious texts, and will generally interpret them hermeneutically, developing a philosophical perspective distinct from conventional religious interpretations. Many forms of mysticism in the modern world will adapt or adopt texts from entirely different faiths - Vivekananda in Vedanta, for instance, is noted for his assertions that all religions are one. As a rule, mysticisms are less concerned with religious differences and more concerned with social or individual development.

What mysticism is most concerned with, however, is having the most effective set of practices to attain enlightened consciousness and union with God. Not much else beyond this matters to a dedicated mystic, who focuses on the inner realms: mind-breath, non-thinking awareness, and so on. Mystics are not too concerned with the opinions or the religious tools of their more conservative religious compatriots.

Process

It is worth mentioning here that Evelyn Underhill outlines the *universal mystic way*, the actual process by which the mystic arrives at union with the absolute. She identifies *five stages of this process*. First is the awakening, the stage in which one begins to have some *consciousness of absolute or divine reality*. The second stage is one of purgation, which is characterized by an *awareness of one's own imperfections and finiteness*. The response in this stage is one of self-discipline and mortification. The third stage, illumination, is one reached by artists and visionaries as well as being the final stage of some mystics. It is marked by a consciousness of a transcendent order and a *vision of a new heaven* and a *new earth*. The great mystics go beyond the stage of illumination to a fourth stage, which Underhill, borrowing the language of St. John of the Cross, calls the dark night of the soul. This stage, experienced by the few, is one of final and complete purification and is marked by confusion, helplessness, stagnation of the will, and a sense of the withdrawal of God's presence. It is the period of final "unselfing" and the surrender to the hidden purposes of the divine will. The final and last stage is one of union with the object of love, the one Reality, God. Here the self has been permanently established on a transcendental level and liberated for a new purpose. Filled up with the Divine Will, it immerses itself in the temporal order, the world of appearances in order to incarnate the eternal in time, to become a mediator between humanity and eternity.

The mystic interprets the world through a different lens than is present in ordinary experience, which can prove to be a significant obstacle to those who research mystical teachings and paths. Much like poetry, the words of mystics are often idiosyncratic and esoteric, can seem confusing and opaque, simultaneously over-simplified and full of subtle meanings hidden from the unenlightened. To the mystic, however, they are pragmatic statements, without subtext or weight; simple obvious truths of experience.

One of the more famous lines from the Tao Te Ching, for instance, reads:

> My words are very easy to know, and very easy to practice;
> but there is no one in the world who is able to know and able to practice them. (Legge, 70)

Remarkably, References to "the world" are common in

mystical and religious traditions, including admonitions to be separate, and the call to a detachment analogous to emptiness. One key to enigmatic expressions lies in the perspective that "the world" of appearances reflects only learned beliefs - based on the limitations of time, culture and relationships - and that unquestioned faith in those misperceptions limits one's return to the divine state. The cloaking of such insights to the uninitiated is an age-old tradition; the malleableness of reality was thought to pose a significant danger to those harboring impurities.

Strategies

Aphorisms, poetry, and etc.

semi-artistic efforts to crystallize some particular description or aspect of the mystical experience in words

- *God is Love* (Christian and Sufi in particular)meaning a spirit force, *Atman is Brahman* (Advaitan), Zen haiku, Rumi's love poems (Sufism). Over time many of these have become trite slogans, losing their core meaning as depictions of practical experience, i.e. "God is Love" - describing the power of creation inherent in pure desire/ unconflicted singlemindedness of will.

Koans, riddles, and metaphysical contradictions

irresolvable tasks or lines of thought designed to direct one away from intellectualism and effort towards direct experience.

- The classic "What is the sound of one hand?" (Zen) (or the more popular variant, "What is the sound of one hand *clapping*?") or "How many angels can stand on the head of a pin?" (Christian). Sometimes these are dismissed as mere incomprehensible silliness (see humor, below); sometimes they are taken as serious questions whose answers would have mystical significance. In either case, the intention is lost; the point being that excessive effort in contemplating the impossible leads the initiate to give up the ego pursuit of doing/getting as opposed to the unity experience of being/having.
- The evocative Taoist phrase - To yield is to be preserved whole, to be bent is to become straight, to be empty is to be full, to have little is to possess - is another example

of a metaphysical contradiction describing the path of emptying of the learned self.

Humor and humorous stories

teachings that simultaneously draw one away from serious discussion and highlight metaphysical points

- Primary examples are the Nasrudin tales, many of which focus on the unreliability of perception, e.g. someone shouts at Nasrudin sitting on a river bank, "How do I get across?" "You are across." he replies; Bektashi jokes, which serve as a means of opposing the pressures put on society by Orthodox Islam, and the Trickster or Animal Spirit stories passed down in Native American, Australian Aboriginal, and African Tribal folklore. Even the familiar "Br'er Rabbit and the Tar Baby", for example, is fairly acute psychology wrapped in a children's tale. Humor of this sort is often corrupted into mere jokes: some Nasrudin tales have a clear metaphysics built in, while others have devolved into little more than depictions of a crazy, dimwitted old man.

Parables and metaphor

stories designed to teach a particular but unconventional metaphysical view of reality indirectly, by using analogy

- One familiar example - the Garden of Eden story of Adam and Eve being cast out in shame - has lost its metaphorical meaning over time; the psychological/ metaphysical consequences of shame when the innocent creative ego (feminine aspect) is tempted to reach for power and subsequently enters the belief in duality (eating of the tree of good and evil) because reason (masculine aspect of mind) has yet to waken. In the story, return to the Garden and Tree of Eternal Aliveness (divine reality) is only possible through purification of mind (the gate is protected by the lone innocent cherubim/Self wielding a flaming sword.) Compare this to the symbols of fire, masculine/feminine unity, time, fearlessness, and ego transcendence found in images of "Shiva the Destroyer" (Hindu) where the transformational process is described by visual metaphors. Christ is well-known for his use of parables, consistently using them to teach compassion and inclusion, while many contain hidden metaphorical content for "those who have ears to hear." In one of the most enigmatic stories from the Gospel of Thomas, he

> describes the Kingdom of Heaven as like an old woman returning home after a long journey, carrying all she values - a bag full of grain - on her back. A tear allows the grain to escape during the journey and she arrives home to discover it empty. Very Buddhist in tone, each word of the story has significance in describing the return path to the divine through a gradual emptying of earthbound value concepts and subtle internal conflicts. The use of the term, old woman, is a common metaphor related to the mind's incapacity to create, when controlled by embedded defensive ego values.

Metaphysics and Philosophy & Sciences

Throughout history and even today mysticism has attempted to gain scientific validity by borrowing from all branches of science various laws, theories, jargon, formula, etc. These are then incorporated into the literature (for example) to give the uninformed reader the feeling that what is being discussed is "scientifically sound" and thus valid. Mysticism is generally considered experiential and holistic, and mystical experiences held to be beyond expression; modern philosophy, psychology, biology and physics sometimes being seen as overtly analytical, verbal, and reductionist. However, in some instances throughout history, mystical and philosophical thought were closely entwined.

Empedocles, Parmenides, Plato and Pythagoras, and to a lesser extent Socrates, had elements in their teachings that could be interpreted as mystical in nature; many of the great Christian mystics were also prominent philosophers, and certainly, for some, Buddha's Sutras and Shankara's 'Crest Jewel of Discrimination' (fundamental texts in Buddhism and Advaitan Hinduism, respectively) display what seem to be analytical treatments of mystical ideas. Baruch de Spinoza, the 17th c. philosopher, while supporting the new discoveries of science and eschewing traditional Jewish concepts of God and miracles, espoused that Nature/ Universe was one holistic reality with the highest virtue -

the power inherent in preserving essence (being) or "conatus," and the highest form of knowledge - the intuitive knowing of the Real. Whether or not these shared understandings occur in the field of philosophy is for students of such subjects or interests to interpret.

The pursuit of knowledge in the realm of physics was sometimes seen as inseparable from understanding the mind of God - the 20th c. comment by Albert Einstein that "God does not play dice," referring to the unfathomable discoveries of quantum physics, is often cited to lend an aura of scientific validity to discussions of a mystical nature. The rift between mysticism and the modern sciences derives mainly from elements of scientism in the latter: certain branches of the natural sciences, sometimes disavow subjective experience as meaningless, fully understanding the limitations of the ancient languages. That said, several areas of study in biology (work of Mae Wan Ho and Lynn Margulis are two examples) and philosophy address the same issues that concern the mystic, and some modern physicists are now attempting to understand a multiple dimensional reality that, coincidentally, philosophers and mystics' have attempted to describe for millennia.

David Bohm speaking of consciousness expressing itself as matter and/or energy could be completely understood by the mystic or philosopher, whatever his cultural/religious heritage. It should be clear that no scientific backing need be used in that understanding but it is sometimes forced together for validity's sake. However, the historical lack of rigor in defining "dimensions" does not make it clear that historical mysticism and philosophical "dimensions" are the same as what physicists are defining.

Furthermore, Continental philosophy tends to be concerned with issues closely related to mysticism, such as the subjective experience of existence in Existentialism. It should be noted that while existentialism suggests a nothingness rather than a oneness, the mystic's pursuit of emptiness - despite its fear producing angst - for the sake of union with the Divine, points directly toward a potential unity between physics and psychology that does not at present exist. The mystic's attempt to describe cause and effect between one's internal state and the miraculous, hints at a close connection between psychological stability (ego transcendence) and the mysterious realm of causality quantum physicists are now deciphering - dimensional reality shifts that synchronize with states of consciousness and unconflicted choices.

Ontology, Epistemology, Phenomenology

It is pertinent to note that while the three philosophical fields - the nature of reality, knowledge and phenomenon - would appear to all relate to aspects of mystical experience, they have not as yet been correlated in a systematic way. Traditional use of the term ontology makes it a synonym of metaphysics. Prior to Immanuel Kant's theoretical separation of "reality" from the "appearance of reality," with human knowledge limited to the latter, the field of ontology/ metaphysics concerned itself with the overall structure or nature of reality. Afterwards, many philosophers separated philosophical and mystical approaches in a seemingly permanent way. 'The general focus on experience in mysticism tends to belie ontological questions; mystical ontology is rarely stated in clear affirmative particulars. Often, it consists of generalized, transcendent identity statements—*"Atman is Brahman", "God is Love", "There is only One without a Second"* — or other phrases suggestive of immanence. Sometimes it is stated in negative terms, from the Hindu tradition for instance, the word Brahman is usually defined as *God 'without' characteristics or attributes*.

Buddhist teachings explicitly discourage ontological beliefs, Taoist philosophy consistently reminds that ontos is knowable but inexpressible, and certain 'psychological' schools—spiritual schools following after Carl Jung, and philosophical schools derived from Husserl—concern themselves more with the transformation of perceptions within consciousness than the connection between transformed consciousness and the external Real. Mysticism is related to epistemology to the extent that both are concerned with the nature, acquisition and limitations of knowledge. However, where epistemology struggles with foundational issues—*how* do we know that our knowledge is true or our beliefs justified—mystics often appear more concerned with process as the means to true knowing. However, every mystical path has necessarily as its ontological purpose, the discernment between truth and illusion, and many approaches emphasize the total discarding of beliefs as the prerequisite to knowledge in the phenomenological sense. Foundational questions are generally answered, in mystical thought, by mystical experiences. Their focus, less on finding procedures of reason that will establish clear relations between ontos and episteme, but rather on finding practices that will yield clear perception. The goals therefore are the same, but the mystic's awareness of evolving levels of consciousness encompass another realm altogether. At least one branch of epistemology claims that non-rational procedures (e.g. statements of desire, random selection, or intuitive processes) are in some cases acceptable means of arriving at beliefs, while the mystic's goal is discarding said beliefs as a limit to knowledge.

The term "mysticism" is also used in a pejorative sense in branches of epistemology to refer to material beliefs that cannot be justified empirically, and thus considered irrational.

> ... we see all religions at their highest point end in mysticism and mysteries, that is to say, in darkness and veiled obscurity. These really indicate merely a blank spot for knowledge, the point where all knowledge necessarily ceases. Hence for thought this can be expressed only by negations, but for sense-perception it is indicated by symbolical signs, in temples by dim light and silence, in Brahmanism even by the required suspension of all thought and perception for the purpose of entering into the deepest communion with one's own self, by mentally uttering the mysterious *Om*. In

> the widest sense, mysticism is every guidance to the immediate awareness of what is not reached by either perception or conception, or generally by any knowledge. The mystic is opposed to the philosopher by the fact that he begins from within, whereas the philosopher begins from without. The mystic starts from his inner, positive, individual experience, in which he finds himself as the eternal and only being, and so on. But nothing of this is communicable except the assertions that we have to accept on his word; consequently he is unable to convince.
>
> – *Schopenhauer, The World as Will and Representation, Vol. II, Ch. XLVIII*

In fact, the emphasis that is placed on subjective direct experience of the "divine and otherworldly transcendent goal of unity", makes it highly controversial to individuals who place a greater emphasis on empirical verification of knowledge and truth (such as scientists for example). In this sense, one again returns to a more philosophical context within the fields of Epistemology and the philosophy of perception, exploring the notions of truth, belief, knowledge and verification.

Phenomenology

Phenomenology is perhaps the closest philosophical perspective to mystical thinking, and shares many of the difficulties in comprehension that plague mysticism itself. Husserl's phenomenology, for instance, insists on the same first-person, experiential stance that mystics try to achieve: his notion of phenomenological *epoché*, or bracketing, precludes assumptions or questions about the extra-mental existence of perceived phenomena.

Heidegger goes a step beyond: rather than merely bracketing phenomena to exclude ontological questions, he asserts that only 'beingness' has ontological reality (similar to Baruch de Spinoza's suppositions) and thus only investigation and experiencing of the self can lead to authentic existence. Christian mystics would assert that "the Kingdom of Heaven is within" references the same approach. Phenomenology and most forms of mysticism part ways, however, in their understanding of the experience. Phenomenology (and in particular existentialist phenomenology) is pre-conditioned by angst (existential dread), which arises from the discovery of the essential emptiness of 'the real' and can go no further; mystics, by contrast take the step beyond to "being" and describe the peace or bliss that derives from their final active connection to 'the Real'. Those who adopt a phenomenological approach to mysticism believe that an argument can be made for concurrent lines of thought throughout mysticism, regardless of interaction.

Remarkably, Ken Wilber who has also studied mysticism and mystical philosophies in some depth comments that:

> "There is nothing spooky or occult about this. We have already seen identity shift from matter to body to mind, each of which involved a decentering or dis-identifying with the lesser dimension... consciousness is simply continuing this process and dis-identifying with the mind itself, which is precisely why it can witness the mind, see the mind, experience the mind. The mind is no longer a subject, it is starting to become an object [in the perception of] the observing self. And so the mystical, contemplative and yogic traditions pick up where the mind leaves off... with the observing self as it begins to transcend the mind."

> "The contemplative traditions are based upon a series of experiments in awareness: what if you pursue this Witness to its source? What if you inquire within, pushing deeper and deeper into the source of awareness itself? What do you find? As a repeatable, reproducible experiment in awareness? One of the most famous answers to that question begins: There is a subtle essence that pervades all reality. It is the reality of all that

is, and the foundation of all that is. That essence is all. That essence is the real. And thou, thou art that. In other words, the observing self eventually discloses its own source, which is Spirit itself, Emptiness itself... and the stages of transpersonal growth and development are basically the stages of following this observing self to its ultimate abode."

Q: "How do you know these phenomena actually exist?

A: "As the observing self begins to transcend... deeper or higher dimensions of consciousness come into focus. All of the items on that list are objects that can be directly perceived in that worldspace. Those items are as real in [that] worldspace as rocks are in the sensorimotor worldspace and concepts are in the mental worldspace. If cognition awakens or develops to this level, you simply perceive these new objects as simply as you would perceive rocks in the sensory world or images in the mental world. They are simply given to awareness, they simply present themselves, and you don't have to spend a lot of time trying to figure out if they're real or not." "Of course, if you haven't awakened to [this] cognition, then you will see none of this, just as a rock cannot see mental images. And you will probably have unpleasant things to say about people who do see them".

In the similar vein, according to Joseph Chilton Pearce, we have transcendence itself as our biological imperative:

"...Spiritual transcendence and religion have little in common. In fact, if we look closely, we can see that these two have been the fundamental antagonists in our history, splitting our mind into warring camps. Neither our violence nor our transcendence is a moral or ethical matter of religion, but rather an issue of biology. We actually contain a built-in ability to rise above restriction, incapacity, or limitation and, as a result of this ability, possess a vital adaptive spirit that we have not yet fully accessed."

"Historically our transcendence has been sidetracked... by our projection of these transcendent potentials rather than our development of them. We project when we intuitively recognize a possibility or tendency within ourselves but perceive this as a manifestation or capacity of some person, force, or being outside of ourselves. We seem invariably to project onto each other our negative tendencies..., while we project our transcendent potentials onto principalities and powers "out there" on cloud nine or onto equally nebulous scientific laws... we wander in a self-made hall of mirrors, overwhelmed by inaccessible reflections of our own mind."

"Culture has been defined by anthropologists as a collection of learned survival strategies passed on to our young through teaching and modeling...as the collected embodiment of our survival ideation, is the mental environment to which we must adapt, the state of mind with which we identify. The nature or character of a culture is colored by the myths and religions that arise within it, and abandoning one myth or religion to embrace another has no effect on culture because it both produces and is produced by these elements...That we are shaped by the culture we create makes it difficult to see that our culture is what must be transcended, which means we must rise above our notions and techniques of survival itself, if we are to survive. Thus the paradox that only as we lose our life do we find it."

"A new breed of biologists and neuroscientists have revealed why we behave in so paradoxical a manner that we continually say one thing, feel something else, and act from an impulse different from either

> of these...A major clue to our conflict is the discovery ...that we have five different neural structures, or brains, within us. These five...represent the whole evolution of life preceding us; reptilian, old mammalian, and human (other two?). Nature never abandons a good idea but instead builds new structures upon it...Thus, while we refer to transcendence in rather mystical, ethereal terms, to the intelligence of life, transcendence may be simply the next intelligent move to make."
>
> "...Neurocardiology, a new field of medical research, has discovered in our heart a major brain center that functions in dynamic with the fourfold brain in our head. Outside our conscious awareness, this heart-head dynamic reflects, determines, and affects the very nature of our resulting awareness even as it is, in turn, profoundly affected."

Theistic, pantheistic, and panentheistic metaphysical systems most often understand mystical experience as individual communion with God. One can receive these very subjective experiences as visions, miracles, dreams, revelations, or prophecies, for example. Going beyond "natural theology" (*theologia naturalis*) to direct experience of God is "mystical theology" (*theologia mystica*) or, as Thomas Aquinas defined it, "experiential knowledge of God" (*cognitio dei experimentalis*). In Catholicism the mystical experience is not sought for its own sake, and is always informed by revelation and ascetical theology. The effort being analogous to reentering a divine "field," which we misperceive we have been excluded - by sin/shame/remorse. Repentance (awareness of lower-self attachments) and ascetics (giving up the thoughts/behaviors) is the requirement for reestablishing divine communion/unity/grace.

Terms descriptive of a desired afterlife include Moksha (*liberation* or *release*), Heaven (traditionally understood as a gathering place for goodly spirits, near to God and other holy beings), and Nirvana (literally *extinguishing* of the mental fetters or *unbinding* of the mind), but in mystical parlance these reference an experience of reality "different from the present here and now." The goal is generally established through an "accidental" revelatory or miraculous experience such as a dimensional shift between one structure of reality to another. Once this "potentiality" has been experienced/received/observed, understanding how and why it has occurred becomes the goal of the individual and permanently stabilizing this "direct experience of God" is obsessively pursued. Because terms descriptive of the divine "goal" are defined differently - even by individuals within a given religion - and their usage within mysticism is often no less imprecise, it is extremely difficult for anyone, who has not experienced the simultaneity of the "shift in awareness/reality" to translate mystical language in a useful way.

Experience

Remarkably, W.T. Stace proposes two common classifications of mystical and religious experiences in his book *Mysticism and Philosophy*:

1. *Extrovertive* – mystical consciousness of the unity of nature overlaid onto one's sense perception of the world.
2. *Introvertive* – any experience that includes sense-perceptual, somatosensory, or introspective content. An experience of "nothingness" or "emptiness", in some mystical traditions, are examples of introvertive experiences.

The Soul and Mysticism

To begin with, Abrahamic religions conceive of a soul that lies within each individual, which is of great spiritual significance. However, Judaism, placing more focus on this world than others, has resulted in multiple views ... that man is a partner in God, all the way to the mystical esoteric knowledge of numerology and the Kabbalah.

Remarkably, Christian mysticism has diverse takes on the relationship between God and the soul with purification and reunion the goal and the soul synonymous with the Christ Self or one's true God-given nature. In Catholicism, saints and other beatific individuals are sometimes said to have received the Holy Spirit — who grants them miraculous, prophetic, or other transcendent abilities — and this belief is taken up in certain charismatic and evangelical faiths that seek out testaments to divine revelation through spontaneous speaking in tongues, faith healing, the casting out of demons, etc. However, the practice is generally unrelated to a disciplined mystical approach. In the Quaker view, the soul is inner light, an inherent presence of God within the individual. Other Christian traditions, such as Catholicism, hold a more distinct division between the individual soul and God, given the traditional belief that the salvation of the soul and union with God will occur only at the resurrection after physical death, but these faiths generally hold that righteousness is possible and necessary during life.

Eastern Orthodoxy holds that union with God happens in this life during baptism and continues via the process of theosis. Christian mystics, such as Jacob Boehme, seek this unity state of the soul while in the body, variously, through intense prayer, ascetism (purification), contemplation and meditation, to achieve resurrection of the Christ Self/nature in this life.

Similarly, the Jainist view of soul is perceivable non-matter that can connect to infinite knowledge, but cannot receive that knowledge without removal of the blanket of karma. However, as self knowledge is gained, the hold of karma is loosened, everything can be seen clearly and nirvana(salvation) is achieved. The pure soul — divine unity — is accomplished when all the power of karma is destroyed.

Islam shares this conception of a distinct soul, but with

less focus on miraculous powers; the Muslim world emphasizes remembrance (dhikr, zikr): the recalling of one's original and innate connection to Allah's grace. In traditional Islam this connection is maintained by angels, who carry out God's will — returning the soul to one's authentic origin — though only prophets have the ability to see and hear them directly. In Islam the mystical path is incorporated within Sufi and the Self/Soul is embattled (jihad) with the infidel/ego. Sufism holds that God can be experienced directly as a universal love that pervades the universe. Remembrance, for Sufis, explicitly means remembrance of the soul's love/purpose or returning to one's original divine state, and Sufis are particularly noted for the artistic turn their forms of worship often take.

In fact, Eastern philosophies, such as Hinduism, Buddhism, and Taoism are concerned with the individual soul's dissolution of ego (moksha) into transcendent reality (generally Brahman or Ishvara). In the mystical aspects of the Vedic tradition Atman (something not entirely different from the western conception of the soul) is believed to be identical with Brahman. Hindu mystical practices, taught in five main Vedantic disciplic successions, primarily aim for *God-consciousness* and eternal life of the liberated soul in varieties of ecstatic loving service of the Godhead. One of the disciplic successions, founded by Sankara, aim at loss of eternal individuality, in oneness with the Godhead.

Buddhist teaching holds that all suffering (dukkha) in the world comes from craving, aversion and ignorance ('raga', 'dosa', 'moha'), and that freedom from suffering comes from the extinction ('nirodha') of these poisons, which are the source of mental defilements ('klesha'), through the development of insight and equanimity. The doctrine of 'anatta' suggests that the perception of an unchanging and cohesive self (the 'me'), is itself a mere mental construct ('vijnana') to which one may be attached, and is thus also a major source of suffering. While Mahayana and Vajrayana Buddhist schools invoke various deities and venerated beings, the mystical sects of Buddhism are generally not concerned with, and even overtly deny, the existence of a permanent or unchanging self, or of a permanent or unchanging deity. There is no term equivalent to the Christian idea of 'soul' in the Buddhist lexicon however belief in rebirth is assumed throughout the Buddhist world.

Taoism is largely unconcerned with the soul. Instead, Taoism centers around the tao ('the way' or 'the path'). The human tendency, according to Taoism, is to conceive of dualisms; the Taoist mystical practice is to recapture and conform with that original unity (called te, de, which is translated as virtue).

Regardless of particular conceptions of the soul, a common thread of mysticism is the experience of a collective peace, joy, compassion or love.

Pantheism

Pantheism means "God is The All" and "All is God". It is the idea that natural law, existence, and/or the universe (the sum total of all that is, was, and shall be) is represented or personified in the theological principle of 'God'.

Acosmism

In contrast Acosmism denies the reality of the universe, seeing it as ultimately illusory (maya), with only the infinite unmanifest Absolute as real.

Dualism

There are also dualist conceptions, often with an evil (though existent) material world of the ego competing with a transcendent and perfect spiritual plane aligned with the true self/essence. Gnosticism is a term for various mystical initiatory religions, sects and knowledge schools that were most active in the first few centuries of the Christian/ Common Era around the Mediterranean and extending into central Asia. These systems typically recommend the pursuit of special knowledge (*gnosis*) as the central goal of life. They also commonly depict creation as a dualistic struggle between competing forces of light and dark, and posit a marked division between the material realm, which is typically depicted as under the governance of malign forces, and the higher spiritual realm from which it is divided. As a result of these traits, dualism, anticosmism and body-hatred are sometimes present within Gnosticism. There is, however, variety, subtlety, and complexity in the traditions involved.

Non-Dualism

Mysticism is often found in common with nondual worldviews and many mystics, from whichever religion or tradition they originally came, also describe in many ways a non-dual view of existence. Ramesh Balsekar comments on nonduality and mysticism, that it is in order for phenomena to occur, that the illusion of personal existence and doership (ego) is present, and explains mysticism and nonduality in fairly accessible (conventional) terms:

> "Consciousness-at-rest is not aware of Itself only the force around it. It becomes aware of Itself only when this sudden feeling, I-am, arises, the impersonal sense of being aware. And that is when Consciousness-at-rest becomes Consciousness-in-movement, Potential energy becomes actual energy. They are not two. Nothing separate comes out of Potential energy becoming the one true being... That moment that science calls the Big Bang, the mystic calls the sudden arising of awareness..."

Syncretism

Related to syncretism, mystics of different traditions report similar experiences of a world/reality outside conventional perception, although this does not infer an abandonment of knowledge understood through normal means. Mystics describe the same unity experience across history, culture and religion - despite the extreme individuality of the experience. If the attempt of religion, philosophy and science to describe reality is comparative to the fable of five blind men attempting to define an elephant by describing its parts, the mystic of every religion and culture sees the elephant despite the individuality of approach and differences in culture and language. Elements of mysticism exist at the core of all religions and in many philosophies, including those where the majority of the followers have no awareness of this. Some mystics perceive a common thread of divine influence in all religions and philosophies.

The Vedic tradition is inherently mystic; the Christian apocalyptic Book of Revelation is clearly mystical, as with Ezekiel's or Daniel's visions of Judaism, and Muslims believe that the angel Gabriel revealed the Qur'an in a miraculous manner. Indigenous cultures also have cryptic revelations pointing toward a universal flow of love or unity, usually following a vision quest or similar ritual. Mystical philosophies thus can exhibit a strong tendency towards syncretism.

Mysticism and Traditional Religions

Conventional religions by definition, are marked by strong institutional structures, including formal hierarchies and mandated sacred texts and/or creeds. Adherents of the faith are expected to respect or follow each of these closely.

Most mystical paths arise in the context of some particular religion but tend to set aside or move beyond these institutional structures, often believing themselves to be following the 'purest' or 'deepest' representations of that faith. Thus, to the extent that a mystical path has a hierarchy, it is generally limited to teacher/student relationships; to the extent that they use a central text or ethical code, they view them as interpretable guidelines rather than established law.

Conventional religious perspectives towards mystics

varies between and within faiths. Sometimes (as with the Catholic church and Vedantic Hinduism), mystics are incorporated into the church hierarchy, with criteria set up for validation of mystical experiences and veneration of those who achieve that status. In other cases, mystical paths follow a separate but parallel course. Traditionally, Buddhist monks were closely interwoven into the fabric of village life through most of Asia, but had no authoritative position in the community; and almost all the traditional Islamic scholars were Sufis, including Al-Shafi'i, Imam Nawawi, and Al-Ghazali.

Some systems of mysticism are found within specific religious traditions and do not relinquish doctrinal principles as a part of mystical experience. In some definite cases, theology remains a distinct source of insight that guides and informs the mystical experience. Some faiths—including most Protestant Christian sects—find mystical practices disreputable; so called mystic "practices" and beliefs generally restricted to specific sects, such as the Religious Society of Friends or certain Charismatic groups, which have implicitly incorporated them.

The mystic's disregard of religious institutional structures often lends a quasi-revolutionary aspect to mystical teaching, and this occasionally leads to conflict with established religious and political structures, or the creation of splinter groups or new faiths. The relation of mysticism to ethics and morality is more complex than is usually assumed. Mystical experiences do not guarantee that mystics will be compassionate or moral, nor on the other hand is a mystical state incompatible with being morally concerned with others. Rather, a given mystic's ethics will depend on the factual beliefs and values espoused in that mystic's religious tradition..

New Religious Movements, Perennial Philosophy and Entheogens

The late 19th century saw a significant increase of interest in mysticism in the West that combined with increased interest in Occultism and Eastern Philosophy. Theosophy became a major movement in the popularization of these interests. Madame Blavatsky functioned as a central figure of the theosophy movement. This trend later became absorbed in the rise of the New Age movement, which included a major surge in the popularity of psychological self-awareness groups such as EST and many others. At the end of the twentieth century books like A Course in Miracles (purported to be a channeled course of study dictated by Jesus) and Conversations with God (in which the author describes his direct communication with God) became popularized.

The term perennial philosophy, coined by Leibniz and popularized by Aldous Huxley, relates to what some take to be the mystic's primary concern:

> [W]ith the one, divine reality substantial to the manifold world of things and lives and minds. But the nature of this one reality is such that it cannot be directly or immediately apprehended except by those who have chosen to fulfill certain conditions, making themselves loving, pure in heart, and poor in spirit.

Some mystics use the term to refer to a manner wherein the mystic strives to plumb the depths of the self and reality in a radical process of meditative self-exploration, with the aim of experiencing the true nature of reality.

In some cultures and traditions, mind-altering substances—often referred to as entheogens—have been used as a guide; the Santo Daime and Uniao do Vegetal being notable modern examples.

It is important to note that many of the self-styled mystical belief systems arising in recent decades essentially differ from mysticism proper in that they rely on the individual seeker's power and will, whereas in the mystic traditions, the states cannot be initiated by the seeker himself, but only by the Ultimate Being. Hence the term *mystikos*. It is also important to note that evidence may exist that suggests entheogen induced experiences was an accepted means to connect with the divine by many religious figures of all the worlds religions.

In Rosicrucianism, Masonry and Golden Dawn

The Rosicrucian Order is a legendary and secretive Order publicly documented in the early 17th century. It is associated with the symbol of the Rose Cross, which is also found in certain rituals beyond "Craft" or "Blue Lodge" Freemasonry. The Rosicrucian Order is viewed among earlier and many modern Rosicrucianists as an inner worlds Order, composed of great "Adepts." When compared to human beings, the consciousness of these Adepts is said to be like that of *demi-gods.* This "College of Invisibles" is regarded as the source permanently behind the development of the Rosicrucian movement.

Freemasonry is a worldwide fraternal organization. Members are said to be joined together by shared ideals of both a moral and metaphysical nature and, in most of its branches, by a constitutional declaration of belief in a Supreme Being. Freemasonry is an esoteric society, in that certain aspects of its internal work are not disclosed to the public, but they claim that it is not an occult system. The private aspects of modern Freemasonry deal with elements of ritual and the modes of recognition amongst members within the ritual.

The Hermetic Order of the Golden Dawn (or Golden Dawn, as it is commonly referred to) is a tradition of magical theurgy and spiritual development, probably the single greatest influence on twentieth century western occultism and many other traditions, including Wicca, Thelema and other forms of magical spirituality popular today. By the mid 1890s, the Golden Dawn was well established in Great Britain, with membership rising to over a hundred from every class of Victorian society. In its heyday, many cultural celebrities belonged to the Golden

Dawn, such as actress Florence Farr, Arthur Machen, William Butler Yeats, Evelyn Underhill and Aleister Crowley. Many men and women of the 19th century Fin de siècle social culture were members of the Golden Dawn.

Mysticism in Buddhism

Buddhism includes a vast array of scriptures, beliefs, traditions and practices. Many of these are not overtly mystical. Yet, some doctrines within Mahayana and Tantric Buddhism have a strong flavour of mysticism. Pre-eminent amongst these are the teachings of Dzogchen and of the Tathagatagarbha. Both of these doctrines indicate the presence of a hidden, deathless core reality within each being—variously called the Buddha Nature, Buddha Matrix, Awakened Mind, Mind Essence, Dzogchen or Mahamudra—which needs to be recognized and 'entered into'. This Essence of Mind is empty of tangible substance and is resistant to the intellect's efforts to conceptualise or 'model' it, but it is supremely Aware and filled with benevolence and compassion. Writing on this theme, Lama Chokyi Nyima Rinpoche explains the Buddha's teaching on the ultimate nature of the Awakened Mind ('bodhicitta'), stating:

> 'What is ultimate bodhicitta? It is truly free from all mental constructs, like space; it cannot be indicated by any analogy whatsoever. It falls into no extreme or category; it is beyond mental constructs. It is the unity of emptiness and compassion; it is empty like space. Yet it is loving and compassionate, open and clear. That is ultimate bodhicitta ...According to Mahamudra, the essence is nonarising, its expression is unceasing, and its manifestation is the unity of these two. According to Dzogchen, the essence is empty, the nature is cognizant or luminous and the compassion is the unity of these two.'

In the same work, Chokyi Nyima writes that the essence of the mind is not a concrete thing, yet is not to be viewed as non-existent; nor is it a multitude of things or just one thing. It is an essence that could be called the 'I' or the Ground of all that is:

> 'It is not found to be a concrete thing ... Yet it is not nonexistent, since your mind is vividly awake. It is not a singularity, because it manifests in manifold ways. Nor is it a plurality, because all these are of one essence. There is no one who can describe its nature ... It may be given many kinds of names such as "mind essence", "I", or the "all-ground". It is the very basis of all of samsara and nirvana.'

Elucidating this notion of the Buddha Nature or Buddha Matrix, Professor Jeffrey Hopkins comments:

> 'The basis [of the spiritual life] is the ground on which the spiritual path acts to rid it of peripheral obstructions, thereby yielding the fruit of practice. The basis is the matrix-of-one-gone-thus [Buddha Nature], which itself is the thoroughly established nature, the uncontaminated primordial wisdom empty of all compounded phenomena – permanent, stable, eternal, everlasting. Not compounded by causes and conditions, the matrix-of-one-gone-thus [Buddha Nature] ... is not something that did not exist before and is newly produced; it is self-arisen.'

One specific mysticism of Buddhism is union with Dharmakaya through jhana. Dharmakaya is both the wisdom body of The Buddha, for one, and is also the omnipresent Mind. This unbegotten and immortal essence within each being is called the Dharma-kaya – Body of Truth – or Buddha Within (as Dr. Shenpen Hookham has termed it Its nature is described in the *Samadhiraja Sutra*, where the Buddha states:

> 'the Body of the Tathagata [i.e. Buddha] should be defined as ... having its essence identical with

Space, invisible, surpassing the range of vision – thus is the Absolute Body to be conceived. Inconceivable, surpassing the sphere of thought, not oscillating between bliss and suffering, surpassing the illusory differentiation, placeless, surpassing the voice of those aspiring to the Knowledge of Buddhi, essential, surpassing passions, indivisible, surpassing hatred, steadfast, surpassing infatuation, explained by the indications of emptiness, unborn, surpassing birth, eternal from the standpoint of common experience, undifferentiated in the aspect of Nirvana, described in words as ineffable, quiescent in voice, homogenous with regard to conventional Truth, conventional with regard to the Absolute Truth – Absolute according to the true teaching.'

2

Origin and Development

Mysticism is a nebulous term. The *Concise Oxford Dictionary* (1911), after defining a mystic as "one who believes in spiritual apprehension of truths beyond the understanding," adds, "whence *mysticism* (n.) (often contempt)." Whatever may be the precise force of the remark in brackets, it is unquestionably true that mysticism is often used in a semi-contemptuous way to denote vaguely any kind of occultism or spiritualism, or any specially curious or fantastic views about God and the universe.

In fact, word itself was originally taken over by the Neo-platonists from the Greek mysteries, where the name of given to the initiate, probably arose from the fact that he was one who was gaining a knowledge of divine things about which he must keep his mouth shut (close lips or eyes). Hence the association of secrecy or "mystery" which still clings round the word. Two facts in connection with mysticism are undeniable whatever it may be, and whatever part it is destined to play in the development of thought and of knowledge. In the first place, it is the leading characteristic of some of the greatest thinkers of the world—of the founders of the Eastern religions of Plato and Plotinus, of Eckhart and Bruno, of Spinoza, Goethe, and Hegel.

Secondly, no one has ever been a lukewarm, an indifferent, or an unhappy mystic. If a man has this particular temperament, his mysticism is the very centre of his being: it is the flame which feeds his whole life; and he is intensely and supremely happy just so far as he is steeped in it.

It is pertinent to note that Mysticism is, in truth, a temper rather than a doctrine, an atmosphere rather than a system of philosophy. Various mystical thinkers have contributed fresh aspects of Truth as they saw her, for they have caught glimpses of her face at different angles, transfigured by diverse emotions, so that their testimony, and in some respects their views, are dissimilar to the point of contradiction. Wordsworth, for instance, gained his revelation of divinity through Nature, and through Nature alone; whereas to Blake "Nature was a hindrance," and Imagination the only reality. But all alike agree in one respect, in one passionate assertion, and this is that unity underlies diversity. This, their starting-point and their goal, is the basic fact of mysticism, which, in its widest sense, may be described as an attitude of mind founded upon an intuitive or experienced conviction of unity, of oneness, of alikeness in all things.

From this source springs all mystical thought, and the mystic, of whatever age or country, would say in the words of Krishna—

> There is true knowledge. Learn thou it is this:
> To see one changeless Life in all the Lives,
> And in the Separate, One Inseparable.
>
> —*The Bhagavad-Gîtâ*, Book 18.

This fundamental belief in unity leads naturally to the further belief that all things about us are but forms or manifestations of the one divine life, and that these phenomena are fleeting and impermanent, although the spirit which informs them is immortal and endures. In other words, it leads to the belief that "the Ideal is the only Real."

Further, if unity lies at the root of things, man must have some share of the nature of God, for he is a spark of the Divine. Consequently, man is capable of knowing God through this godlike part of his own nature, that is, through his soul or spirit. For the mystic believes that as the intellect is given us to apprehend material things, so the spirit is given us to apprehend spiritual things, and that to disregard the spirit in spiritual matters, and to trust to reason is as foolish as if a carpenter, about to begin a piece of work, were deliberately to reject his keenest and sharpest tool. The methods of mental and spiritual knowledge are entirely different. For we know a thing mentally by looking at it from outside, by comparing it with other things, by analysing and defining it, whereas we can know a thing spiritually only by becoming it. We must *be* the thing itself, and not merely talk about it or look at it. We must be in love if we are to know what love is; we must be musicians if we are to know what music is; we must be godlike if we are to know what God is. For, in Porphyry's words: "Like is known only by like, and the condition of all knowledge is that the subject should become like to the object."

So that to the mystic, whether he be philosopher, poet, artist, or priest, the aim of life is to become like God, and thus to attain to union with the Divine. Hence, for him, life is a continual advance, a ceaseless aspiration; and reality or truth is to the seeker after it a vista ever expanding and charged with ever deeper meaning. John Smith, the Cambridge Platonist, has summed up the mystic position and desire in one brief sentence, when he says, "Such as men themselves are, such will God Himself seem to them to be." For, as it takes two to communicate the truth, one to speak and one to hear, so our knowledge of God is precisely and accurately limited by our capacity to receive Him. "Simple people," says Eckhart, "conceive that we are to see God as if He stood on that side and we on this. It is not so: God and I are one in the act of my perceiving Him."

This sense of unity leads to another belief, though it is one not always consistently or definitely stated by all mystics. It is implied by Plato when he says, "All knowledge is recollection." This is the belief in pre-existence or persistent life, the belief that our souls are immortal, and no more came into existence when we were born than they will cease to exist when our bodies disintegrate. The idea is familiar in Wordsworth's *Ode on the Intimations of Immortality*.

Finally, the mystic holds these views because he has lived through an experience which has forced him to this attitude of mind. This is his distinguishing mark, this is what differentiates him alike from the theologian, the logician, the rationalist philosopher, and the man of science, for he bases his belief, not on revelation, logic, reason, or demonstrated facts, but on *feeling*, on intuitive inner knowledge.

He has felt, he has seen, and he is therefore convinced; but his experience does not convince any one else. The mystic is somewhat in the position of a man who, in a world of blind men, has suddenly been granted sight, and who, gazing at the sunrise, and overwhelmed by the glory of it, tries, however falteringly, to convey to his fellows what he sees. They, naturally, would be sceptical about it, and would be inclined to say that he is talking foolishly and incoherently. But the simile is not altogether parallel. There is this difference. The mystic is not alone; all through the ages we have the testimony of men and women to whom this vision has been granted, and the record of what they have seen is amazingly similar, considering the disparity of personality and circumstances. And further, the world is not peopled with totally blind men. The mystics would never hold the audience they do hold, were it not that the vast majority of people have in themselves what William James has called a "mystical germ" which makes response to their message.

James's description of his own position in this matter, and his feeling for a "Beyond," is one to which numberless "unmystical" people would subscribe. He compares it to a tune that is always singing in the back of his mind, but which he can never identify nor whistle nor get rid of. "It is," he says, "very vague, and impossible to describe or put into words.... Especially at times of moral crisis it comes to me, as the sense of an unknown something backing me up. It is most indefinite, to be sure, and rather faint. And yet I know that if it should cease there would be a great hush, a great void in my life."

This sensation, which many people experience vaguely and intermittently, and especially at times of emotional exaltation, would seem to be the first glimmerings of that secret power which, with the mystics, is so finely developed and sustained that it becomes their definite faculty of vision. We have as yet no recognised name for this faculty, and it has been variously called "transcendental feeling," "imagination," "mystic reason," "cosmic consciousness," "divine sagacity," "ecstasy," or "vision," all these meaning the same thing. But although it lacks a common name, we have ample testimony to its existence, the testimony of the greatest teachers, philosophers, and poets of the world, who describe to us in strangely similar language—

That serene and blessed mood
In which ... the breath of this corporeal frame,
And even the motion of our human blood,
Almost suspended, we are laid asleep
In body, and become a living soul:
While with an eye made quiet by the power

Of harmony, and the deep power of joy, We see into the life of things. *Tintern Abbey.*

"Harmony" and "Joy," it may be noted, are the two words used most constantly by those who have experienced this vision.

The mystic reverses the ordinary methods of reasoning: he must believe before he can know. As it is put in the

Theologia Germanica, "He who would know before he believeth cometh never to true knowledge." Just as the sense of touch is not the faculty concerned with realising the beauty of the sunrise, so the intellect is not the faculty concerned with spiritual knowledge, and ordinary intellectual methods of proof, therefore, or of argument, the mystic holds, are powerless and futile before these questions; for, in the words of Tennyson's Ancient Sage—

> Thou canst not prove the Nameless, O my son,
> Nor canst thou prove the world thou movest in:
> Thou canst not prove that thou art body alone,
> Nor canst thou prove that thou art spirit alone,
> Nor canst thou prove that thou art both in one:
> Thou canst not prove thou art immortal, no,
> Nor yet that thou art mortal—nay, my son,
> Thou canst not prove that I who speak with thee
> Am not thyself in converse with thyself,
> For nothing worthy proving can be proven,
> Nor yet disproven.

Symbolism is of immense importance in mysticism; indeed, symbolism and mythology are, as it were, the language of the mystic. This necessity for symbolism is an integral part of the belief in unity; for the essence of true symbolism rests on the belief that all things in Nature have something in common, something in which they are really alike. In order to be a true symbol, a thing must be partly the same as that which it symbolises. Thus, human love is symbolic of divine love, because, although working in another plane, it is governed by similar laws and gives rise to similar results; or falling leaves are a symbol of human mortality, because they are examples of the same law which operates through all manifestation of life. Some of the most illuminating notes ever written on the nature of symbolism are in a short paper by R. L. Nettleship, where he defines true mysticism as "the consciousness that everything which we experience, every 'fact,' is an element and only an element in 'the fact'; i.e. that, in being what it is, it is significant or symbolic of more."

In short, every truth apprehended by finite intelligence must by its very nature only be the husk of a deeper truth, and by the aid of symbolism we are often enabled to catch a reflection of a truth which we are not capable of apprehending in any other way. Nettleship points out, for instance, that bread can only be itself, can only *be* food, by entering into something else, assimilating and being assimilated, and that the more it loses itself (what it began by being) the more it "finds itself" (what it is intended to be). If we follow carefully the analysis Nettleship makes of the action of bread in the physical world, we can see that to the man of mystic temper it throws more light than do volumes of sermons on what seems sometimes a hard saying, and what is at the same time the ultimate mystical counsel, "He that loveth his life shall lose it."

It is worth while, in this connection, to ponder the constant use Christ makes of nature symbolism, drawing the attention of His hearers to the analogies in the law we see working around us to the same law working in the spiritual world. The yearly harvest, the sower and his seed, the leaven in the loaf, the grain of mustard-seed, the lilies of the field, the action of fire, worms, moth, rust, bread, wine, and water, the mystery of the wind, unseen and yet felt—each one of these is shown to contain and exemplify a great and abiding truth.

This is the attitude, these are the things, which lie at the heart of mysticism. In the light of this, nothing in the world is trivial, nothing is unimportant nothing is common or unclean. It is the feeling that Blake has crystallised in the lines:

> To see a world in a grain of sand
> And a Heaven in a wild flower,

Hold Infinity in the palm of your hand
And Eternity in an hour.

The true mystic then, in the full sense of the term, is one who *knows* there is unity under diversity at the centre of all existence, and he knows it by the most perfect of all tests for the person concerned, because he has felt it. True mysticism—and this cannot be over-emphasised—is an experience and a life. It is an experimental science, and, as Patmore has said, it is as incommunicable to those who have not experienced it as is the odour of a violet to those who have never smelt one. In its highest consummation it is the supreme adventure of the soul: to use the matchless words of Plotinus, it is "the flight of the Alone to the Alone."

As distinguished, therefore, from the mystical thinker or philosopher, the practical mystic has direct knowledge of a truth which for him is absolute. He consequently has invariably acted upon this knowledge, as inevitably as the blind man to whom sight had been granted would make use of his eyes.

Among English writers and poets the only two who fulfil this strict definition of a mystic are Wordsworth and Blake. But we are not here concerned primarily with a study of those great souls who are mystics in the full and supreme sense of the word. For an examination of their lives and vision Evelyn Underhill's valuable book should be consulted. Our object is to examine very briefly the chief English writers—men of letters and poets—whose inmost principle is rooted in mysticism, or whose work is on the whole so permeated by mystical thought that their attitude of mind is not fully to be understood apart from it.

Naturally it is with the poets we find the most complete and continuous expression of mystical thought and inspiration. Naturally, because it has ever been the habit of the English race to clothe their profoundest thought and their highest aspiration in poetic form. We do not possess a Plato, a Kant, or a Descartes, but we have Shakespeare and Wordsworth and Browning. And further, as the essence of mysticism is to believe that everything we see and know is symbolic of something greater, mysticism is on one side the poetry of life. For poetry, also, consists in finding resemblances, and universalises the particulars with which it deals. Hence the utterances of the poets on mystical philosophy are peculiarly valuable. The philosopher approaches philosophy directly, the poet obliquely; but the indirect teaching of a poet touches us more profoundly than the direct lesson of a moral treatise, because the latter appeals principally to our reason, whereas the poet touches our "transcendental feeling." So it is that mysticism underlies the thought of most of our great poets, of nearly all our greatest poets, if we except Chaucer, Dryden, Pope, and Byron. Shakespeare must be left on one side, first, because the dramatic form does not lend itself to the expression of mystical feeling, and secondly, because even in the poems there is little real mysticism, though there is much of the fashionable Platonism.

Shakespeare is metaphysical rather than mystical, the difference being, roughly, that the metaphysician seeks to know the beginnings or causes of things, whereas the mystic feels he knows the end of things, that all nature is leading up to union with the One. We shall find that mystical thought, and the mystical attitude, are curiously persistent in English literature, and that although it seems out of keeping with our "John Bull" character, the English race has a marked tendency towards mysticism. What we do find lacking in England is the purely philosophical and speculative spirit of the detached and unprejudiced seeker after truth. The English mind is anti-speculative; it cares little for metaphysics; it prefers theology and a given authority. English mystics have, as a rule, dealt little with the theoretical side of mysticism, the aspect for instance with which Plotinus largely deals. They have been mainly practical mystics, such as William Law. Those of the poets who have consciously had a system and desired to impart it, have done so from the practical point of view, urging, like Wordsworth, the importance of contemplation and meditation, or, like Blake, the value of cultivating the imagination; and in both cases enforcing the necessity of cleansing the inner life, if we are to become conscious of our divine nature and our great heritage. For the sake of clearness, this thought may first be traced very briefly as it appears chronologically; it will, however, be considered in detail, not in order of time, but according to the special aspect of Being through which the writer felt most in touch with the divine life. For mystics, unlike other thinkers, scientific or philosophical, have little chronological development, since "mystic truths can neither age nor die." So much is this the case that passages of Plotinus and Tennyson, of Boehme and Law, of Eckhart and Browning, may be placed side by side and be scarcely distinguishable in thought. Yet as the race evolves, certain avenues of sensation seem to become more widely opened up.

This is noticeable with regard to Nature. Love, Beauty, Wisdom, and Devotion, these have been well-trodden paths to the One ever since the days of Plato and Plotinus; but, with the great exception of St Francis of Assisi and his immediate followers, we have to wait for more modern times before we find the intense feeling of the Divinity in Nature which we associate with the name of Wordsworth. It is in the emphasis of this aspect of the mystic vision that English writers are supreme. Henry Vaughan, Wordsworth, Browning, Richard Jefferies, Francis Thompson, and a host of other poet-seers have crystallised in immortal words this illuminated vision of the world. The thought which has been described as mystical has its roots in the East, in the great Oriental religions. The mysterious "secret" taught by the Upanishads is that the soul or spiritual consciousness is the only source of true knowledge. The Hindu calls the soul the "seer" or the "knower," and thinks of it as a great eye in the centre of his being, which, if he concentrates his attention upon it, is able to look outwards and to gaze upon Reality. The soul is capable of this because in essence it is one with Brahman, the universal soul. The apparent separation is an illusion wrought by matter.

Hence, to the Hindu, matter is an obstruction and a deception, and the Eastern mystic despises and rejects and subdues all that is material, and bends all his faculties on realising his spiritual consciousness, and dwelling in that. This type of thought certainly existed to some extent in both Greece and Egypt before the Christian era. Much of Plato's thought is mystical in essence, and that which be points out to be the motive force of the philosophic mind is also the motive force of the mystic, namely, the element of attraction, and so of love towards the thing which is akin to him. The illustration of the dog being philosophic because he is angry with a stranger but welcomes his friend, though at first it may seem, like many of Plato's illustrations, far-fetched or fanciful, in truth goes to the very root of his idea. Familiarity, akinness, is the basis of attraction and affection. The desire of wisdom, or the love of beauty, is therefore nothing but the yearning of the soul to join itself to what is akin to it.

This is the leading conception of the two great mystical dialogues, the Symposium and the Phædrus. In the former, Socrates, in the words of the stranger prophetess Diotima, traces the path along which the soul must travel, and points out the steps of the ladder to be climbed in order to attain to union with the Divine. From beauty of form and body we rise to beauty of mind and spirit, and so to the Beauty of God Himself. He who under the influence of true love rising upward from these begins to see that beauty, is not far from the end. And the true order of going or being led by another to the things of love, is to use the beauties of earth as steps along which he mounts upwards for the sake of that other beauty, going from one to two, and from two to all fair forms, and from fair forms to fair practices, and from fair practices to fair notions, until from fair notions he arrives at the notion of absolute beauty, and at last knows what the essence of beauty is. This ... is that life above all others which man should live, in the contemplation of beauty absolute. That is a passage whose music re-echoes through many pages of English literature, especially in the poems of Spenser, Shelley, and Keats.

In fact, Plato may therefore be regarded as the source of speculative mysticism in Europe, but it is Plotinus, his disciple, the Neo-platonist, who is the father of European mysticism in its full sense, practical as well as speculative, and who is also its most profound exponent. Plotinus (A.D. 204-270), who was an Egyptian by birth, lived and studied under Ammonius Sakkas in Alexandria at a time when it was the centre of the intellectual world, seething with speculation and schools, teachers and philosophies of all kinds, Platonic and Oriental, Egyptian and Christian. Later, from the age of forty, he taught in Rome, where he was surrounded by many eager adherents. He drew the form of his thought both from Plato and from Hermetic philosophy (his conception of Emanation), but its real inspiration was his own experience, for his biographer Porphyry has recorded that during the six years he lived with Plotinus the latter attained four times to ecstatic union with "the One." Plotinus combined, in unusual measure, the intellect of the metaphysician with the temperament of the great psychic, so that he was able to analyse with the most precise dialectic, experiences which in most cases paralyse the tongue and blind the discursive reason.

His sixth Ennead, "On the Good or the One," is one of the great philosophic treatises of the world, and it sums up in matchless words the whole mystic position and experience. There are two statements in it which contain the centre of the writer's thought. "God is not external to any one, but is present in all things, though they are ignorant that he is so." "God is not in a certain place, but wherever anything is able to come into contact with him there he is present" (*Enn.* vi. 9, §§ 4, 7). It is because of our ignorance of the indwelling of God that our life is discordant, for it is clashing with its own inmost principle. We do not know ourselves. If we did, we would know that the way home to God lies within ourselves. "A soul that knows itself must know that the proper direction of its energy is not outwards in a straight line, but round a centre which is within it" (*Enn.* vi. 9, § 8).

The whole Universe is one vast Organism (*Enn.* ix. 4, §§ 32, 45), and the Heart of God, the source of all life, is at the centre, in which all finite things have their being, and to which they must flow back; for there is in this Organism, so Plotinus conceives, a double circulatory movement, an eternal out-breathing and in-breathing, the way down and the way up. The way down is the out-going of the undivided "One" towards manifestation. From Him there flows out a succession of emanations.

The first of these is the "Nous" or Over-Mind of the Universe, God as thought. The "Mind" in turn throws out an image, the third Principle in this Trinity, the Soul of all things. This, like the "Nous," is immaterial, but it can act on matter. It is the link between man and God, for it has a lower and a higher side. The lower side *desires* a body and so creates it, but it is not wholly incarnate in it, for, as Plotinus says, "the soul always leaves something of itself above."

From this World Soul proceed the individual souls of men, and they partake of its nature. Its nature is triple, the animal or sensual soul, closely bound to the body, the logical reasoning human soul, and the intellectual soul, which is one with the Divine Mind, from whence it comes and of which it is an image. Souls have forgotten then: divine origin because at first they were so delighted with their liberty and surroundings (like children let loose from their parents, says Plotinus), that they ran away in a direction as far as possible from their source. They thus became clogged with the joys and distractions of this lower life, which can never satisfy them, and they are ignorant of their own true nature and essence. In order to return home, the soul has to retrace the path along which she came, and the first step is to get to know herself, and so to know God. Thus only can she be restored to the central unity of the universal soul.

This first stage on the upward path is the purgative life, which includes all the civic and social virtues, gained through general purification, self-discipline, and balance, with, at the same time, a gradual attainment of detachment from the things of sense, and a desire for the things of the spirit. The next step is to rise up to mind (*Enn.* v. 1, § 3) to the world of pure thought, the highest unity possible to a self-conscious being. This is often called the illuminative life, and it might be summed up as concentration of all the faculties—will, intellect, feeling—upon God. And lastly comes the unitive life, which is contemplation, the intense desire of the soul for union with God, the momentary foretaste of which has been experienced by many of the mystics.

This last stage of the journey home, the supreme Adventure, the ascension to the One above thought, this cannot be spoken of or explained in words, for it is a state beyond words, it is "a mode of vision which is ecstasy." When the soul attains to this state, the One suddenly appears, "with nothing between," "and they are no more two but one; and the soul is no more conscious of the body or of whether she lives or is a human being or an essence; she knows only that she has what she desired, that she is where no deception can come, and that she would not exchange her bliss for the whole of Heaven itself".

The influence of Plotinus upon later Christian mysticism was immense, though mainly indirect, through the writings of two of his spiritual disciples, St Augustine (354-450), and the unknown writer, probably of the early sixth century, possibly a Syrian monk, who ascribes his works to Dionysius the Areopagite, the friend of St Paul. The works of "Dionysius" were translated from Greek into Latin by the great Irish philosopher and scholar, John Scotus Erigena (Eriugena), and in that form they widely influenced later mediæval mysticism.

The fusion of Eastern mysticism with Christianity finally brought about the great change which constitutes the difference between Eastern and Western mysticism, a change already foreshadowed in Plato, for it was in part the natural outcome of the Greek delight in material beauty, but finally consummated by the teachings of the Christian faith. Eastern thought was pure soul-consciousness, its teaching was to annihilate the flesh, to deny its reality, to look within, and so to gain enlightenment. Christianity, on the other hand, was centred in the doctrine of the Incarnation, in the mystery of God the Father revealing Himself in human form. Hence the human body, human love and relationships became sanctified, became indeed a means of revelation of the divine, and the mystic no longer turned his thoughts wholly inwards, but also outwards and upwards, to the Father who loved him and to the Son who had died for him. Thus, in the West, mystical thought has ever recognised the deep symbolism and sacredness of all that is human and natural, of human love, of the human intellect, and of the natural world. All those things which to the Eastern thinker are but an obstruction and a veil, to the Western have become the very means of spiritual ascent. The ultimate goal of the Eastern mystic is summed up in his assertion, "I am Brahman," whereas the Western mystic believes that "he who sees the Infinite in all things, sees God."

In the twelfth and thirteenth centuries the mystical tradition was carried on in France by St Bernard (1091-1153), the Abbot of Clairvaux, and the Scotch or Irish Richard of the Abbey of St Victor at Paris, and in Italy, among many others, by St Bonaventura (1221-1274), a close student of Dionysius, and these three form the chief direct influences on our earliest English mystics.

England shares to the full in the wave of mystical experience, thought, and teaching which swept over Europe in the fourteenth and early fifteenth centuries, and at first the mystical literature of England, as also of France, Germany, Italy, and Sweden, is purely religious or devotional in type, prose treatises for the most part containing practical instruction for the inner life, written by hermits, priests, and "anchoresses." In the fourteenth century we have a group of such writers of great power and beauty, and in the work of Richard Rolle, Walter Hilton, Julian of Norwich, and the author of the *Cloud of Unknowing*, we have a body of writings dealing with the inner life, and the steps of purification, contemplation, and ecstatic union which throb with life and devotional fervour.

From the time of Julian of Norwich, who was still alive in 1413, we find practically no literature of a mystical type until we come to Spenser's *Hymns* (1596), and these embody a Platonism reached largely through the intellect, and not a mystic experience. It would seem at first sight as if these hymns, or at any rate the two later ones in honour of Heavenly Love and of Heavenly Beauty, should rank as some of the finest mystical verse in English. Yet this is not the case. They are saturated with the spirit of Plato, and they express in musical form the lofty ideas of the *Symposium* and the *Phædrus*: that beauty, more nearly than any other earthly thing, resembles its heavenly prototype, and that therefore the sight of it kindles love, which is the excitement and rapture aroused in the soul by the remembrance of that divine beauty which once it knew. And Spenser, following Plato, traces the stages of ascent traversed by the lover of beauty, until he is caught up into union with God Himself. Yet, notwithstanding their melody and their Platonic doctrine, the note of the real mystic is wanting in the *Hymns*, the note of him who writes of these things because he knows them.

It would take some space to support this view in detail. Any one desirous of testing it might read the account of transport of the soul when rapt into union with the One as given by Plotinus (*Enn.* vi. 9, § 10), and compare it with

Spenser's description of a similar experience (*An Hymne of Heavenly Beautie*, 11. 253-273). Despite their poetic melody, Spenser's words sound poor and trivial. Instead of preferring to dwell on the unutterable ecstasy, contentment, and bliss of the experience, he is far more anxious to emphasise the fact that "all that pleased earst now seemes to paine."

The contradictory nature of his belief is also arresting. In the early part of the *Hymne of Heavenly Beautie*, in-speaking of the glory of God which is so dazzling that angels themselves may not endure His sight, he says, as Plato does,

> The meanes, therefore, which unto us is lent
> Him to behold, is on his workes to looke,
> Which he hath made in beauty excellent.

This is the view of the true mystic, that God may be seen in all His works, by the eye which is itself purified. Yet, in the last stanza of this beautiful Hymn, this is how Spenser views the joy of the union of the soul with its source, when it looks

> at last up to that Soveraine Light,
> From whose pure beams al perfect beauty springs,
> That kindleth love in every godly spright
> Even the love of God; *which loathing brings*
> *Of this vile world and these gay-seeming things.*

This is not the voice of the mystic. It is the voice of the Puritan, who is also an artist, who shrinks from earthly beauty because it attracts him, who fears it, and tries to despise it. In truth, the dominating feature in Spenser's poetry is a curious blending of Puritanism of spirit with the Platonic mind.

In the seventeenth century, however, England is peculiarly rich in writers steeped in mystical thought.

First come the Quakers, headed by George Fox. This

rediscovery and assertion of the mystical element in religion gave rise to a great deal of writing, much of it very interesting to the student of religious thought. Among the *Journals* of the early Quakers, and especially that of George Fox, there are passages which charm us with their sincerity, quaintness, and pure flame of enthusiasm, but these works cannot as a whole be ranked as literature. Then we have the little group of Cambridge Platonists, Henry More, John Smith, Benjamin Whichcote, and John Norris of Bemerton. These are all Platonic philosophers, and among their writings, and especially in those of John Norris, are many passages of mystical thought clothed in noble prose. Henry More, who is also a poet, is in character a typical mystic, serene, buoyant, and so spiritually happy that, as he told a friend, he was sometimes "almost mad with pleasure." His poetical faculty is, however, entirely subordinated to his philosophy, and the larger portion of his work consists of passages from the *Enneads* of Plotinus turned into rather obscure verse. So that he is not a poet and artist who, working in the sphere of the imagination, can directly present to us mystical thoughts and ideas, but rather a mystic philosopher who has versified some of his discourses. At this time also many of the "metaphysical poets" are mystical in much of their thought. Chief among these is John Donne, and we may also include Henry Vaughan, Traherne, Crashaw, and George Herbert.

Bunyan might at first sight appear to have many of the characteristics of the mystic, for he had certain very intense psychic experiences which are of the nature of a direct revelation of God to the soul; and in his vivid religious autobiography, *Grace Abounding*, he records sensations which are akin to those felt by Rolle, Julian, and many others. But although psychically akin, he is in truth widely separated from the mystics in spirit and temperament and belief. He is a Puritan, overwhelmed with a sense of sin, the horrors of punishment in hell, and the wrath of an outside Creator and Judge, and his desire is aimed at escape from this wrath through "election" and God's grace.

But he is a Puritan endowed with a psychopathic temperament sensitive to the point of disease and gifted with an abnormally high visualising power. Hence his resemblance to the mystics, which is a resemblance of psychical temperament and not of spiritual attitude.

In the eighteenth century the names of William Law and William Blake shine out like stars against a dark firmament of "rationalism" and unbelief. Their writings form a remarkable contrast to the prevailing spirit of the time. Law expresses in clear and pointed prose the main teachings of the German seer Jacob Boehme; whereas Blake sees visions and has knowledge which he strives to condense into forms of picture and verse which may be understood of men. The influence of Boehme in the eighteenth and nineteenth centuries is very far-reaching. In addition to completely subjugating the strong intellect of Law, he profoundly influenced Blake. He also affected Thomas Erskine of Linlathen, and through him, Carlyle, J. W. Farquhar, F. D. Maurice, and others. Hegel, Schelling, and Schlegel are alike indebted to him, and through them, through his French disciple St Martin, and through Coleridge—who was much attracted to him—some of his root-ideas returned again to England in the nineteenth century, thus preparing the way for a better understanding of mystical thought. The Swedish seer Emmanuel Swedenborg (1688-1772) was another strong influence in the later eighteenth and the nineteenth centuries. Swedenborg in some ways is curiously material, at any rate in expression, and in one point at least he differs from other mystics. That is, he does not seem to believe that man has within him a spark of the divine essence, but rather that he is an organ that reflects the divine life. He is a recipient of life, but not a part of life itself. God is thought of as a light or sun outside, from which spiritual heat and light (= love and wisdom) flow into men. But, apart from this important difference Swedenborg's thought and teaching are entirely mystical. He believes in the substantial reality of spiritual things, and that the most essential part of a person's nature, that which he carries with him into the spiritual world, is his love. He teaches that heaven is not a place, but a condition, that there is no question of outside rewards or punishments, and man makes his own heaven or hell; for, as Patmore pointedly expresses it—

> Ice-cold seems heaven's noble glow
> To spirits whose vital heat is hell.

He insists that Space and Time belong only to physical life, and when men pass into the spiritual world that love is the bond of union, and thought or "state" makes presence, for thought is act. He holds that instinct is spiritual in origin; and the principle of his science of correspondences is based on the belief that everything outward and visible corresponds to some invisible entity which is its inward and spiritual cause. This is the view echoed by Mrs Browning more than once in *Aurora Leigh*—

> There's not a flower of spring,
> That dies in June, but vaunts itself allied
> By issue and symbol, by significance
> And correspondence, to that spirit-world
> Outside the limits of our space and time,
> Whereto we are bound.

In all this and much more, Swedenborg's thought is mystical, and it has had a quite unsuspected amount of influence in England, and it is diffused through a good deal of English literature.

Blake knew some at least of Swedenborg's books well; two of his friends, C. A. Tulk and Flaxman, were devoted Swedenborgians, and he told Tulk that he had two different states, one in which he liked Swedenborg's writings, and one in which he disliked them. Unquestionably, they sometimes irritated him, and then he abused them, but it is only necessary to read his annotations of his copy of Swedenborg's *Wisdom of the Angels* (now in the British

Museum) to realise in the first place that he sometimes misunderstood Swedenborg's position and secondly, that when he did understand it, he was thoroughly in agreement with it, and that he and the Swedish seer had much in common.

Coleridge admired Swedenborg, he gave a good deal of time to studying him (see Coleridge's letter to C. A. Tulk, July 17, 1820), and he, with Boehme, were two of the four "Great Men" unjustly branded, about whom he often thought of writing a "Vindication" (Coleridge's Notes on Noble's Appeal, *Collected Works*, ed. Shedd, 1853 and 1884, vol. v. p. 526).

Emerson owes much to Swedenborg, and Emerson's thought had much influence in England. Carlyle also was attracted to him (see his letter from Chelsea, November 13, 1852); Mrs Browning studied him with enthusiasm and spent the winter of 1852-3 in meditation on his philosophy (*Letters*, vol. ii. p. 141), which bore fruit four years later in *Aurora Leigh*. Coventry Patmore is, however, the English writer most saturated with Swedenborg's thought, and his *Angel in the House* embodies the main features of Swedenborg's peculiar views expressed in *Conjugial Love*, on sex and marriage and their significance.

It is not too much to say that Swedenborg influenced and coloured the whole trend of Patmore's thought, and that he was to him what Boehme was to Law, the match which set alight his mystical flame. He says Swedenborg's *Heaven and Hell* "abounds with perception of the truth to a degree unparalleled perhaps in uninspired writing," and he asserts that he never tires of reading him, "he is unfathomably profound and yet simple." Whatever may be the source or reason, it is clear that at the end of the eighteenth century we begin to find a mystical tinge of thought in several thinkers and writers, such as Burke, Coleridge, and Thomas Erskine of Linlathen. This increases in the early nineteenth century, strengthened by the influence, direct and indirect, of Boehme, Swedenborg, and the German transcendental philosophers and this mystical spirit is very marked in Carlyle, and, as we shall see, in most of the greatest nineteenth-century poets.

Beside those writers which are here dealt with in detail, there is much of the mystic spirit in others of the same period, to name a few only, George Meredith, "Fiona Macleod," Christina Rossetti, and Mrs Browning; while other writers like "A. E.," W. B. Yeats, and Evelyn Underhill were carrying on the mystic tradition.

Mysticism is still in use though fragmentally in English literature writing.

3
Medieval Mysticism

First it is significant to note that by c. 1250, Mysticism flourished in many parts of Europe, including Germany, Italy, the Low Countries, and England, from the middle of the thirteenth century to the middle of the fifteenth. The greatest figures in Germany were Meister Eckhart, a Dominican friar of formidable intellectual gifts, and his pupils, also Dominicans, Johannes Tauler and Henry Suso. In the Low Countries, John Ruusbroec developed a Trinitarian mysticism that owed much to Eckhart, despite his apparent disagreement with the earlier teacher. In Italy, the Franciscan scholar Bonaventure, St. Catherine of Siena, and St. Catherine of Genoa upheld the mystical flame, and there was also a mystical outpouring in England, associated with the names Julian of Norwich, Richard Rolle, Walter Hilton, and the anonymous author of The Cloud of Unknowing.

Remarkably, many of the continental mystics were members of the Friends of God, a movement that worked for the spiritual revival of people at a time when the worldliness of the Catholic Church, the ravages of the Black Death, and the cracks in the traditional social order created a desire in many to develop a deeper spirituality. Although some of the mystics were hermits, like Rolle, others combined their mysticism with practical concerns such as preaching, administrative duties, and caring for the poor and the sick. The most enduring figures in medieval mysticism produced works of high spiritual and sometimes even literary quality. Although they were all loyal to the Church (including Eckhart, in spite of the fact that he was posthumously condemned for heresy), they expressed their mysticism in a wide variety of themes and tones. Eckhart's lofty statements from the standpoint of eternity are very different from Catherine of Genoa's intense dialogue between soul and body, for example. Similarly, the visions of Christ's passion granted to Julian of Norwich differ greatly from the down-to-earth advice given by the author of The Cloud of Unknowing. Taken as a whole, the writings of the medieval mystics provide a remarkable record of the vitality and variety of the spirituality of the period.

REPRESENTATIVE AUTHORS

Bonaventure (1217-1274)

Bonaventure was born Giovanni di Fidanza in Bagnoregio, Italy, around the year 1217. He entered the Franciscan order and was later sent to Paris to complete his education. In Paris he became friends with Thomas Aquinas, one of the great philosophers in the Christian tradition. Bonaventure taught in Paris from 1248 to 1257, when he was elected minister general of the Franciscan Order. He held this position for sixteen years, during which time he wrote his major works, including Life of Francis, a biography of St. Francis of Assisi, and The Soul's Journey into God. Bonaventure was made a cardinal in 1273; he died the following year, on July 15, while attending the Second Council of Lyons. He was canonized in 1482 and declared a Doctor of the Church by Pope Sixtus V in 1587.

Catherine of Genoa (1447-1510)

Catherine of Genoa was born in 1447 to an aristocratic family. She had a melancholy temperament, which was made more pronounced by an unhappy marriage. A powerful spiritual experience in 1473 transformed her life, and after a period of penance and prayer she began to work among the city's sick and poor. In 1477, she founded the first hospital in Genoa and was its director from 1490 to 1496. It was during this period, in the summer of 1493, that an outbreak of the plague killed nearly four out of five of those who remained in the city. Catherine herself contracted the disease but recovered. Catherine attracted many followers, and between 1499 and 1507, she discussed her spiritual experiences with them, including the times in which she had experienced union with God. Catherine died on September 15, 1510, and was canonized by Pope Clement XII in 1733.

Catherine of Siena (1347-1380)

Catherine of Siena was born in Siena on March 25, 1347, the twenty-fourth child in a lower-class family. Even as a child she exhibited a longing for God, and she refused to marry. When she was about sixteen, she joined the Mantellate, a Dominican body that worked with the poor and the sick. In spite of her lack of formal education, Catherine also became known as a teacher. During her lifetime she attracted a large following, and she also founded a convent. Catherine was active in politics, acting as ambassador between the Papacy and the city-state of Florence. Throughout her life she had unusual spiritual experiences, including visions and ecstasies. In 1368, she experienced a "mystical marriage" to Christ, after which she felt totally given to Christ. She also received the stigmata (the marks of the wounds of Christ). All her life, Catherine practiced severe penance, and often she would eat very little. In 1380, she was unable to eat at all, which led to her death at the age of thirty-three on April 29 of that year, in Rome, Italy. In 1970, Pope Paul VI proclaimed her a Doctor of the Roman Catholic Church.

Meister Eckhart (c. 1260-c. 1327)

Meister Johann Eckhart, who is widely considered to be the greatest of all the German medieval mystics, was born in the village of Hochheim, near Gotha, Germany in

1260. His father was the steward of a knight's castle in the Thuringian forest. When Eckhart was about fifteen, he entered the Dominican monastery at Erfurt and remained there for at least nine years. He then studied in Cologne before becoming prior of Erfurt and vicar of Thuringia. In about 1300, he was sent to Paris to teach, where he presented the Dominican theological positions against their rivals, the Franciscans. In 1302, the prestigious Studium Generale in Paris conferred a Master's degree on him, and since then he has been known as Meister Eckhart.

In 1303, he became Provincial of the Dominican order in Saxony, and four years later, Vicar of Bohemia. In 1313, Eckhart, now widely known and respected, lived in Strasbourg, where he preached and was prior of a convent. At some later time, not earlier than 1322, he was invited to take up a professorship at the Studium Generale in Cologne, an extremely high honor. But the Archbishop of Cologne harbored a dislike of all mysticism, and in 1327, he formally charged Eckhart with heresy. Eckhart denied the charges and made a vigorous defense. He is believed to have died the following year. In 1329, Pope John XXII condemned many aspects of Eckhart's teaching as heretical.

Julian of Norwich (c. 1342-c. 1416)

There is little information about the life of Julian of Norwich, who was one of the most important figures in medieval English mysticism. She reveals something of herself in her Revelations of Divine Love. She reports that she was given her revelations in 1373, when she was thirty and a half, which would mean she was born in 1342. Since she is named as a beneficiary in a will dated 1416, it appears that she was still living at that time as a recluse in Norwich, supported by the church of St. Julian and St. Edwards in Conisford. This church belonged to the Benedictine community. Julian's writings show her to be well read in many of the classic texts of Christian spirituality, and it is possible that she acquired her education by entering a religious order, although whether she was in fact a nun is not known.

Margery Kempe (c. 1373-c. 1440)

Margery Kempe was born in King's Lynn, Norfolk, England, around 1373. Her father was a prominent civic authority-wool merchant, mayor, and member of Parliament at various times. She married John Kempe around 1393 and they had 14 children together. Immediately after the birth of her first child, Kempe became ill and had a vision of Jesus Christ. Inspired, Kempe recovered and tried to live a more reverent life but for years was tempted by many sins. Resolved to turn her life to God, she undertook a series of pilgrimages to holy sites around Europe and the Middle East. The Book of Margery Kempe details her travels and conversations with God over a forty-year period. During her lifetime, Kempe was charged and cleared several times for violating rules such as preaching in public, which was forbidden to women, and wearing white, which was forbidden to married women. Kempe is last heard of in the historical record in 1438 and died sometime after this date.

Richard Rolle (c. 1300-1349)

Richard Rolle, who was born around 1300 in the Yorkshire region of England, has been called the father of English mysticism. Rolle was a prolific author in both English and Latin and was widely read and admired in his day. He was born at Thornton Dale, near Pickering, in Yorkshire. He studied at Oxford but appears to have abandoned his studies, since he did not receive a degree. Rolle then withdrew from the world and devoted himself to a contemplative life. He had a number of unusual psychic and spiritual experiences, feeling heat in his chest and hearing heavenly music. Some of his acquaintances thought him mad. He described these experiences in Incendium Amoris (c. 1340, trans. The Fire of Love). Rolle's works are characterized by a love of Christ and especially the power of the divine name Jesus. He emphasized love and a religion of the heart. Rolle died in 1349 at Hampole, near Doncaster. Legend has it that he died after tending to victims of the Black Death.

John Ruusbroec (1293-1381)

John Ruusbroec was born in 1293, in the village of Ruusbroec, near Brussels. He became a priest in 1317, when he was twenty-four. For the next twenty-six years he served as chaplain to the church of St. Gudule in Brussels. During this time he wrote treaties opposing the heretical teachings of a woman named Bloemardinne. In 1343, he retired to Groenendael in the forest a few miles from the city with two companions to lead a more solitary life. The small group acquired a few more members and became, with the blessings of the local bishop, an official religious community—canons regular of St. Augustine. Ruusbroec spent the remaining years of his life at Groenendael, where he wrote the most influential of his mystical works. He died December 2, 1381.

Henry Suso (1295-1366)

Henry Suso, who with Eckhart and Tauler was one of the three great figures in German medieval mysticism, was born on March 21, 1295, to a noble family. When he was thirteen his parents sent him to the Dominican friary in the town of Constance. After being a member of the Dominican order for five years, he underwent a conversion experience that became the basis for his later life. In 1322 or 1323, he was sent to pursue advanced studies in the Dominican house at Cologne, an honor given to only a few. There he expanded his knowledge of theology and scripture, and his teacher for some of this period was probably Meister Eckhart. Suso remained in Cologne until 1326 or 1327, when he returned to the friary at Constance as a director of studies for the students in the order. Around 1330, Suso was summoned to Maastricht to defend himself against charges of heresy, and he was dismissed from his position at the friary. But he must have emerged unscathed from the accusations, since later he was appointed prior or superior of the house at Constance. He also preached in the countryside and supervised the spiritual studies of Dominican nuns. In about 1348, Suso was transferred to the Dominican house in Ulm, where he lived for the rest of his life. During this time, he edited his works for publication, collecting them under the title Exemplar. Suso died in Ulm on January 25, 1366.

Johannes Tauler (c. 1300-1361)

Johannes Tauler was born around 1300 to a well-to-do family in Strasbourg. He began training in the Dominican Order in 1314, and became a preacher and director. In 1339, he moved to Basle because that city sided with Pope John XXII in his dispute with Louis of Bavaria, whereas Strasbourg was loyal to Louis. Tauler remained in Basle for four or five years, where his influence in the spiritual movement known as the Friends of God increased. Tauler was a disciple of Eckhart and a friend of Suso. Tauler became widely known in the vicinity for his preaching, and his teaching has survived in modern times in the form of sermons. He died in 1361, in the monastery of Saint Nicholas in Undis, during an outbreak of the plague.

REPRESENTATIVE WORKS

The Book of Margery Kempe

The Book of Margery Kempe was composed in the fifteenth century by an English woman who went on a series of pilgrimages following a sick-bed vision of Jesus Christ. Kempe traveled to holy sites in Jerusalem, Rome, Norway, and Santiago de Compostela, an autonomous community in northwest Spain. She also toured England to visit the religious dignitaries of her era, including Julian of Norwich and Henry Chichele, the Archbishop of Canterbury. She probably could not read; her book was composed by scribes to whom she dictated the text. The Book of Margery Kempe is controversial because Kempe was a middle-class married woman and not a member of a religious order like her revered contemporary female mystic, Julian of Norwich may have been. To this day, some do not consider Kempe's visions to be inspired by the Holy Spirit but, rather, the hallucinations of a mad woman. Her book was not discovered until 1934 and likely only survives because it was not available for destruction during England's Reformation in the early sixteenth century.

The Cloud of Unknowing

The Cloud of Unknowing is an anonymous devotional book written in England, probably in the East Midlands, in the latter part of the fourteenth century. It is one of the classics of the English mystical tradition. The author appears to have been a male priest, but nothing more is known of him. In seventy-five short chapters, the author offers guidance to the spiritual seeker in his quest to know God. He points out that God is calling the disciple to a higher spiritual life. This is an act of grace on the part of God, and the seeker must respond with a desire for God. He must empty his mind of all thoughts and images in order to penetrate the "cloud of unknowing" that stands between him and God. Thoughts must be pushed way in a "cloud of forgetting." Then the love of God may pierce the cloud. Although the process may be difficult, the seeker eventually loses all awareness of himself, and his soul becomes united with God.

The Exemplar

The Exemplar is the title given by Suso to the collection of his own works that he prepared for publication around the mid-fourteenth century. It includes an autobiography, The Life of a Servant, which for the modern reader is the most accessible of Suso's works. Suso describes the severe bodily penance he imposed on himself as well as the visions and mystical experiences that came to him on his spiritual journey. The Exemplar contains three other works. Little Book of Eternal Wisdom was written to rekindle the love for God in those who wish for it, through the examples of Christ's sufferings and the sorrows of the Virgin. Little Book of Truth is about how to live a detached life and touches on many of the most important themes in German mysticism: spiritual freedom, the nature of true discernment, and of union with God. Little Book of Letters consists of letters of instruction for practical life and worship sent by Suso to women under his spiritual direction.

The Fire of Love

In fact, *The Fire of Love* is a translation of a Latin work, Incendium Amoris, written by English mystic Richard Rolle in about 1340. Rolle's devotional text was inspired by the mystical experience he describes in the prologue and chapter fifteen. Sitting in a chapel one day, he felt his own heart burning with heat and heard heavenly music. The experience became the basis of Rolle's poetic exposition of a life lived in what he called the fire of everlasting love. He explains that divine illumination has three aspects: fervor(heat), dulce (sweetness), and canor (song). The heat in the heart he associates with the burning of divine love. Sweetness refers to the peace and joy that results when the heart burns in love and the presence of the divine beloved is felt. By song, Rolle seems to mean the harmony experienced in the individual mind when all its powers are wedded to God; every thought becomes like a melodious song. These three modes of functioning (heat, sweetness, and song) represent the highest perfection of the Christian religion, although Rolle continually warns that they are not easily attained.

4

Western Mysticism: An Overview*

Introduction

As the title of the chapter suggests, here we are concerned with Western Mysticism upto 1770.

The people and movements on this list are arranged chronologically, rather than alphabetically. It is by no means complete in reflecting mystical figures or texts in the West — there are literally hundreds of these. I have simply included writers and texts that seem to me to reflect the high points of mystical writing. They do not represent a single tradition of mysticism.

The biography I give for each of these is intended only to identify the person. If "influences" are mentioned, they are only to try to identify major precursors to a particular person's mystical thought. We have also included a section in which useful terms, important trends, and influential movements are briefly outlined.

Pre-christian Mystics and Influences on Mysticism

Pythagoras (c.580/570-c.500 B.C.E.): A Presocratic philosopher. Founder of a major school of philosophy/religion that emphasized the mystical interconnections in numbers, nature, and the human soul. The natural and the ethical world were inseparable.

---

* Courtesy: Bruce B. Janz, University of Florida.

Parmenides (c.515-c.450 B.C.E.): On Nature, extant in fragments. Another of the Presocratics. Extends Pythagoras by insisting that all that exists is unchanging and unified. Therefore, if something is changing, it is illusory. This paves the way for the two-world view important for much mysticism. Influences: Pythagoras.

Plato (428-348 B.C.E.): Sophist, Republic, Parmenides, many others. Most important of ancient philosophers. His philosophical system provides the basis of most later mystical forms. Influences: Pythagoras, Parmenides.

Aristotle (384-322 B.C.E.): Metaphysics, De Anima, Nicomachean Ethics. While Aristotle himself is not really considered to be a mystic, he is an important influence on later mystics, especially when combined with Plato by Plotinus, and also when Christianized in the high Middle Ages.

Philo (c.20 B.C.E.-c.41 C.E.): The Contemplative Life. An Alexandrian Jew who drew from Platonist tradition, Stoicism, and neo-Pythagoreanism to create a fusion of the active or virtuous life and the contemplative life.

Plotinus (c.205-270 C.E.): Enneads. The non-Christian, neo-Platonic basis for much Christian, Jewish, and Islamic mysticism. Influences: Plato, Aristotle.

Porphyry (c.232-304 C.E.): Isagoge. Compiled Plotinus' Enneads, and wrote a life of Plotinus. He was strongly anti-Christian, yet he became important in the history of Christian mysticism.

Proclus or Proclusthe Lycian (412-485 C.E.): The Elements of Theology. Athenian Neo-platonist, who influenced Pseudo-Dionysius, and beyond him most of the mystical tradition. While respecting Plotinus, Proclus also amended his philosophical structure.

Christian Mystics and Movements

(1) Early Church

Ignatius of Antioch (c. 35-c.107): Christocentric mystic.

For him Christ's death and resurrection take on mystical significance.

St. Polycarp (c.69-c.155): Had a mystical vision which foretold his martyrdom by fire.

Justin Martyr (c.105-c.165): First Apology. Used Greek philosophy as the stepping-stone to Christian theology. The mystical conclusions that some Greeks arrived at, pointed to Christ. Influences: Pythagoras, Plato, Plotinus, Aristotle, Stoicism.

Irenaeus (c.125-c.202): Revolution and Overthrow of False Knowledge (or Against Heresies). Irenaeus' work was directed against Gnosticism. He emphasized John's gospel, particularly the Logos, which became the voice of God that revealed itself to all people.

Tertullian (c.155-c.222): To Martyrs, Apology, Against the Valentinians, Against Marcion, On the Soul. Emphasized a faith that was a contradiction to reason. "I believe because it is absurd." First to use trinitarian (three-in-one) formulation for God.

Origen (c.185-254): On Principles, Against Celsus. Studied under Clement of Alexandria, and probably also Ammonius Saccus (Plotinus' teacher). He Christianized and theologized neo-Platonism. Each soul has individually fallen (emanation), and must find its way back to God (return) through the help of the Logos, Christ. Origen looks quite Gnostic at times.

St. Antony (c.251-356): The Letters of St. Antony the Great. Early hermit or solitary monk, and a model for later monasticism, particularly of his eremetical type.

St. Athanasius (c.296-373): Against the Gentiles, Apology Against the Arians. Bishop of Alexandria (328-73), wrote a Life of Antony, and was an influence on later Eastern Orthodox mysticism.

Gregory of Nazianzus (329-389): Forty-five Sermons. One of the Cappadocians, early church fathers.

Basil the Great (c.330-379): Longer Rules, Liturgy of St. Basil. One of the Cappadocians, early church fathers. He gave a mystical orientation to the monastic movement.

Gregory of Nyssa (c.335-c.398): Dialogue with his Sister Macrina concerning the Resurrection. Believed that the universe existed as a harmonious order emanating from God. One of the Cappadocians.

Augustine (354-430): De Trinitate, Confessions. Important source for much mediaeval mysticism. Brings Platonism and Christianity together. He emphasizes the soul's search for God, made possible by the illumination of the mind of God. Influences: Plato, Plotinus.

(2) Mediaeval (Catholic and Orthodox) Church

Pseudo-Dionysius the Areopagite (writing c.500): The Celestial Hierarchy, the Mystical Theology, and The Divine Names. Originates the distinction between kataphatic and apophatic theology. Influences: Plotinus.

John Scotus Eriugena (c.810-c.877): Periphyseon. Eriugena translated Pseudo-Dionysius from Greek into Latin. He holds that humans are a microcosm of the universe. That which is shared, the essence of all things, is God. Influences: Plotinus, Augustine, Pseudo-Dionysius.

Bernard of Clairvaux (1091-1153): Sermons, De diligendo Deo, On the Love of God. Cistercian mystic. Promoted a mystical vision of rhapsodic love, in which the Church is described in erotic terms as the bride of Christ. His love-mysticism had the tendency to be anti-intellectual, as in his disputes with Abelard.

William of St.-Thierry (c.1085-1148): Golden Letter, On the Contemplation of God, On the Nature and Dignity of Love. A Cistercian contemporary of Bernard's, William also emphasized love-mysticism, but with subtle differences from Bernard in his use of Augustine.

Hildegard of Bingen (1098-1179): Scivias, The Book of Divine Works, Letters. Early German speculative mystic, reminiscent of Isaiah or Ezekiel at times. She was greatly respected in her time, both for her writings as well as for her music and art. Influences: Augustine, Bernard of Clairvaux.

Victorines: Hugh of St. Victor (c.1096-c.1142), Richard of St. Victor (d. 1173): On Sacraments. Hugh is the more important of the two. He argues for a close tie between reason and mysticism.

Francis of Assisi (John Bernardone) (1182-1226): Canticle of the Sun. Founder of the Franciscan order, which emphasized self-renunciation and poverty. Francis approaches nature mysticism at times, particularly when he sees God in all living things.

Albertus Magnus (1206-1280): The teacher of Thomas Aquinas. In the tradition of Pythagoras, emphasized the essential unity of science and mysticism. Influences: Augustine, Pseudo-Dionysius.

Beatrice of Nazareth (1200-1268): The Seven modes of Sacred Love. Belgian Cistercian mystic. Associated with the Beguines. Influences: Augustine.

Mechthild of Magdeburg (1207-1282): The Flowing Light of the Godhead. Strongly feminine images in mysticism. Devotional mystic. Associated with the Beguines. Influences: Bernard of Clairvaux, Hildegard, Gregory the Great.

Bonaventure (John Fidanza) (1217-1274): The Mind's Road to God, The Tree of Life, The Life of St. Francis. Franciscan monk, and the architect of the philosophical, theological, and mystical side of Francis' thought. Mysticism in the Augustinian tradition. Influences: Augustine, St. Francis of Assisi, Victorines.

St. Thomas Aquinas (1224-1275): Summa Theologica, De Anima, many others. Dominican monk and the greatest Catholic theologian and philosopher. Late in life, he had a mystical experience which caused him to question his scholastic past. Influences: Aristotle, Augustine, Pseudo-Dionysius, Eriugena.

Ramon Llull (c.1235-1315): Great Art, The Book of the Lover and the Beloved. Franciscan. Legend has it that Llull wrote 200 works, was an alchemist and a magician. He also worked on the logic of science. The "Great Art" is the scientific and mystical calculation of the interrelations of all things. Influences: Bonaventure.

Angela of Foligno (c.1248-1309): The Book of Divine Consolations of the Blessed Angela of Foligno. Mysticism is based on the facts of Christ's life and death. Influences: Francis of Assisi, Bonaventure.

Marguerite Porete (d. 1310): The Mirror of Simple Souls.

Meister Eckhart (1260-1327/8): Sermons, Parisian Questions and Prologues. [Some English-language selections from his writings are available.] Dominican monk. One of the most important early German speculative mystics. Eckhart is the first of the so-called "Rhineland" mystics. The Sermons were in German, the academic works in Latin. Influences: Pseudo-Dionysius.

Hadewijch (Adelwip) of Brabant/Antwerp (13th century): Letters, Poems in Stanzas, Visions, Poems in Couplets. Belgian Beguine. One of the greatest exponents of love mysticism. Influences: Plato, Plotinus, Pseudo-Dionysius, Gregory of Nyssa, Richard of St. Victor.

Jan van Ruysbroeck (1293-1381): The Adornment of the Spiritual Marriage (Spiritual Espousals), The Sparkling Stone, The Book of Supreme Truth. Flemish mystic, sometimes considered one of the Rhineland mystics. Outlines the stages of the mystical life. Influences: Eckhart, Hadewijch.

Henry Suso (1295-1366): The Little Book of Truth, The Little Book of Wisdom (Horologium·Sapientiae). A Rhineland mystic. Influences: Eckhart.

Gregory Palamas (1296-1359): Eastern Orthodox mystic. Influences: Pseudo-Dionysius, Athanasius.

Johannes Tauler (1300-1361): Sermons. Rhineland mystic and Dominican. Tauler emphasized the inner person rather than outer works, and because of this became popular in Protestant circles in the Reformation, and later Pietism and Romanticism. He was part of the same community that produced the Theologia Germanica. Influences: Eckhart, Mechthild of Magdeburg.

Anonymous (c.1350-1400): Theologia Germanica or Theologia Deutsch. Important influence in the German mystical tradition. Luther rediscovered and popularized it. Influences: Augustine, Eckhart, Tauler.

Richard Rolle (1300-1349): The Fire of Love. Part of the "English school" of late mediaeval mysticism. Emphasizes the "physicality" of the mystical experience (feeling heat, seeing colours, etc.).

Birgitta (Brigida) Suecica of Sweden (1302-1373): Ascetic mystic. Heavily involved in political activity. Influences: St. Francis of Assisi.

Anonymous (c.1349-c.1395): The Cloud of Unknowing, [as modernized, see also early text] The Book of Privy Council. Part of the "English school" of late mediaeval mysticism. The emphasis on "unknowing" God is part of Pseudo-Dionysius' apophatic theology. Influences: Pseudo-Dionysius.

Walter Hilton (d. 1395): The Scale (Ladder) of Perfection, Epistle to a Devout Man. An Augustinian monk, Hilton was an English mystic.

Julian of Norwich (1342-1413?): Showings or

Revelations of Divine Love. Julian was part of the "English school" of late mediaeval mysticism. Mystical experience that came at the point of death. The experience came with healing, and she devoted her life to understanding her vision. Influences: Pseudo-Dionysius, Aquinas (?).

Margery Kempe (c.1413): Mainly known as the biographer of Julian of Norwich.

Catherine of Siena (1347-1380): Il Dialogo. Italian. Mystic; advisor to Pope Gregory XI. Influences: Augustine.

Thomas à Kempis (c.1380-1471): The Imitation of Christ. Augustinian monk. Finest expression of devotio moderna, modern spirituality, which downplays the Rhineland mystics' concern with contemplation and speculative theology, and stresses the practice of simple piety and asceticism. Influences: Eckhart.

Nicolaus of Cusa (Cusanus, Nikolaus Krebs) (1401-1464): The Vision of God (1453), De Docta Ignorantia. German mystic. Part of the revival of Platonism in the Renaissance. Cusanus was a speculative mystic who emphasized the incomprehensibility and paradoxicality of God. Influences: Plotinus, Pseudo-Dionysius, Eckhart.

St. Catherine of Genoa (1447-1510): Life and Doctrines, Treatise on Purgatory. Mysticism spurred in part by the abuse and neglect by her husband. Her trauma becomes mystical as she argues that purgatory is a stage on the mystical path, the final purification of the effects of self-love.

Teresa of Avila (1515-1582): Life, by Herself; The Way of Perfection; The Interior Castle. Spanish Carmelite nun. Formed the Discalced (Barefoot) Carmelites, with St. John of the Cross. Is very important for describing the stages of the mystical journey. Influences: Augustine.

St. John of the Cross (Juan de Yepes) (1542-1591): Dark Night of the Soul and Ascent of Mt. Carmel. Spanish mystic. (Discalced Carmelite) Both John and Teresa emphasize mysticism as union with God, attainable only in the denial of the self. Influences: Teresa of Avila.

Giordano Bruno (1548-1600): Hermetic philosopher, one of the most important philosophers of the Renaissance. Bruno advocated a kind of nature mysticism which had a strong scientific component to it.

St. Francois de Sales (1567-1622): The Introduction to the Devout Life (Philothea), Treatise on the Love of God. French mystic. Devout Life is a classic of French spirituality.

Louis Claude de Saint Martin (1743-1803): Theosophic Correspondence. While technically Catholic, St. Martin's mysticism follows much closer in the tradition of Boehme and other nature mystics. Influences: Boehme, Swedenborg, Weigel, Law.

(3) Non-Catholic Christian Mystics (16th-18th century)

Martin Luther (1483-1546): While Luther had a well-known antipathy to mystics, it is also true that there is the foundation of mystical life in his theology of the heart, particularly in his early thought. Influences: Augustine, Theologica Germanica.

Heinrich Cornelius Agrippa von Nettesheim (1486-1535): De Occulta Philosophia (1533). It is not clear whether to call Agrippa Catholic or not. He did not embrace the Reformation, yet many of his themes are much closer to Weigel and Boehme than to any Catholic mystic. His was a speculative mysticism, as much interested in magic and alchemy as in spiritual life.

Paracelsus (Phillipus Aureolus Theophrastus Bombastus von Hohenheim) (1493-1541): Another speculative mystic more interested in medical alchemy, astronomy, and natural philosophy.

Valentin Weigel (1533-1588): Know Thyself (1572). Weigel begins in the tradition of Rhineland mysticism, and moves to the speculative nature mysticism of Paracelsus. Influences: Eckhart, Tauler, Theologica Germanica, Paracelsus.

Jacob Boehme (1575-1624): Aurora (1612) [in German], Mysterium Pansophicum (1620), Signature Rerum (1622), Mysterium Magnum (1623). Lusatian Lutheran. A major figure in German mysticism. Influences: Eckhart, the Jewish Kabbalah, Valentin Weigel, Renaissance alchemy, Paracelsus.

Christian Knorr von Rosenroth (1636-1689): Kabbala Denudata: The Kabbalah Uncovered. A Christian Kabbalist. Influenced by the Kabbalah, Jacob Boehme.

Angelus Silesius (Johannes Scheffler 1624-1677): The Cherubic Wanderer [Hungarian version] (1657-on). Mysticism in epigrammatic couplets.

George Fox (1624-1691): Founder of the Quakers. Influences: Boehme.

Gottfried Wilhelm Leibnitz (1646-1716): Monadology. Usually thought of as a rationalist philosopher rather than a mystic. However, while it may be too much to call him a mystic, it is certainly possible to see the affinities between his thought and that of Cusanus, Weigel, Boehme, and other nature mystics. His most important contribution is to blend inner life with rationality; most Pietists (and most scientists) assumed them to be mutually exclusive.

William Law (1686-1761): The Spirit of Love (1752-1754). English mystic. Law is most famous for his devotional works (like A Serious Call to a Devout and Holy Life), but later in his life he became interested in Jacob Boehme, and wrote several mystical treatises.

Emanuel Swedenborg (1688-1772): Many works,

including Arcana Coelestia, Heaven and Hell, The Heavenly City, Divine Love and Wisdom, etc. Swedenborg worked out a detailed understanding of nature mysticism, applying it to everything from the animal world to the spiritual world. He is one of the few mystics to have an active following to the present.

Friedrich Christoph Oetinger (1702-1782): Nature mystic, Pietist. Influences: Boehme, Weigel, Swedenborg.

Johann Gottfried Herder (1744-1803): Another person who is often not counted as a mystic, but who followed Leibnitz in attempting to blend science and mysticism into a kind of vitalism. Influences: Cusanus, Boehme, Leibnitz.

NOTE: After the 18th century, the influence of mysticism explodes in the Romanticism of Germany, England, and America. True mystics, however, remain few.

Jewish Mystics and Mysticism

Kabbalah

Abraham ben Samuel Abulafia (1240-1291): One of the founders of the Spanish Kabbalah.

Moses ben Shem Tob de Leon (1250-1305): Zohar (The Book of Splendor). The most important writer of the most important Kabbalist document.

Moses Cordovero (1522-1570): Pardes Rimmonim, Elimah Rabbati, Palmtree of Deborah. Spanish Kabbalist. Cordovero laid the groundwork for the Kabbalist ethical literature that proliferated in the 16th-18th centuries.

Isaac Luria (1534-1572): Founder of the Lurianic Kabbalah, which is the modern version. Most modern Kabbalists follow Luria's version.

Hasidism

Israel ben Eliezer, Ba'al Shem Tov (Besht) (1700-

1760): Founder of the Hasidim, the sect appearing during the final stages of the Kabbalah's development.

Rabbi Nachman of Breslov in the Ukraine (1772-1810): Martin Buber, the author of I and Thou (Ich und Du), calls him the last Jewish mystic.

Islamic Mystics and Mysticism

Sufism has sources in sacred texts, the remembrance of Allah, and respect for those who exemplify the straight path of Islam through and beyond explicit injunctions of the law.

Hasan of Basra (d. 728): Early advocate of ascetic piety. Hasan emphasized the Koran or Qur'an as the standard of right and wrong, which in turn emphasized the fear of God.

al Hallaj (d. 922): The Ta wa-sin Tried and executed for claiming that God had come to dwell in him.

al Farabi (ca. 873-950): Important philosopher as well as a mystic. Influences: Plotinus.

al Ghazali (d. 1111): First-rate Aristotelean philosopher, who extended Aristotle's theory of perception to argue for a kind of mystical perception that goes beyond reason. Influences: Aristotle.

Main Terms, Trends, and Movements

Alchemy: Alchemy, as often as not, assumes a Hermetic world view. Most people know alchemy as the search for the principle of transmutation of baser metals into higher (e.g., lead into gold). It is really broader, and represents the attempt to understand the connections in the world. Paracelsus practiced a medical alchemy, in which the body was a collection of balancing principles, and illness meant that the balance was off. If you take away the spiritual assumptions behind the alchemical forces, you have something remarkably close to Newtonian physics.

Beghards: male counterparts to the Beguines. Fewer, and less of an issue for the church at the time.

Beguines: group of female contemplatives, some of whom were mystics. They were condemned as heretics because they represented a challenge to the church's authority. Many important female mystics were associated with the Beguines, although the group was not necessarily mystical (some thought that mystical visions got in the way of practical life).

Gnosticism: Derived from Greek gnosis, knowledge. The Gnostic is one who claims esoteric knowledge about God and the metaphysical structure of the universe. There is a strong distinction between spirit and matter, God and the world. This position sometimes resulted in asceticism (the spirit must be liberated from the bonds of the flesh), and sometimes antinomianism (the material world is inconsequential, so there is no point in resisting carnal impulses). Some later mysticism (e.g. quietism) has the world-denying aspects of gnosticism.

Hermeticism: Followers of the legendary figure Hermes Trismegistus, or thrice-great Hermes, reputed to be an Egyptian writer. Much nature mysticism of the Renaissance found hermetic thought useful, because both understood the world to be intrinsically interconnected, and only understandable once those connections were understood. Hermes mixed with Pseudo-Dionysius was common fare in Renaissance Italy, until Isaac Casaubon showed that Hermes was not who he said he was.

Kabbalah: Jewish mysticism that has its roots earlier than Christianity, but which flourishes in the Middle Ages and Renaissance. The Kabbalah struggles with the problem of how the human person can relate to a God who is totally other, and how that God relates to creation.

Monasticism: Although the tendency to live apart for spiritual devotion has a long history, it is closely tied to mysticism in the Middle Ages. The disciplines associated with mysticism have their most rigorous application there. The most famous orders are the Franciscans (St. Francis of Assisi, Bonaventure), the Dominicans (Thomas Aquinas, Meister Eckhart), the Carmelites (Teresa of Avila, St. John of the Cross), the Benedictines (St. Benedict), and the Jesuits (St. Ignatius of Loyola). The orders exist to this day, and continue to be places that encourage mysticism and contemplation (Thomas Merton was a Trappist monk, for instance).

Rhineland Mysticism: The Rhineland mystics were German mystics that follow the influence of Meister Eckhart. They tend to emphasize the search for the inner ground of the soul.

Sufism: The mystical bent in Islam is supported by passages from the Koran (or Qur'an) and is represented by the Sufis. Because there is a dominant emphasis on prophetic activism and legalism in Islam, Muslim tradition may be misunderstood as entirely inhospitable to mysticism. But the Sufi way, mainly transmitted through "lay orders" that trace their origin to some influential spiritual teacher, preserve a distinctively Islamic mysticism. Among these Sufi subtraditions are the Naqshbandi and the Nimatullahi, but there are several others. A few modern organizations (such as the International Sufi Movement led by Hidayat Inayat Khan) claim descent from traditional Sufis but do not require their followers to be Muslims. And recently the great Sufi poet Jalaluddin Rumi has been rediscovered as a source of inspiration by poets Robert Bly and Coleman Barks. However, most practicing Sufis affirm that they are Muslims.

Important Secondary Sources

The secondary sources in mysticism are quite varied. Sometimes whole works are devoted to the subject; sometimes chapters of quite unexpected works will be on mysticism. More general reflections on mysticism can be found as introductions or appendices to works on particular mystics or chapters in philosophies or psychologies of religion. And, many works on mysticism that seem to be reflections on the nature of mysticism turn out to be anthologies of writings of various mystics. Compounding the problem is the fact that the word "mysticism" has been used for all sorts of experiences, philosophical positions, personality types, writings, or whatever. Where to go?

Well, here are my favorites. Of course, this is highly selective, not to mention somewhat idiosyncratic. I will start with the good general bibliographies first — consulting these will lead you to other things. You will have to find bibliographies for individual mystics yourself (come see me on this; I might be able to help). In the "General Secondary Sources" section, I have not included several fine works that reflect on mysticism in general from the point of view of a particular mystic (except for von Huegel's work, that is). Most of these you can find by looking for the particular mystic.

REFERENCES

Bowman, Mary Ann. *Western mysticism: A guide to the basic works.*

Carmody, Denise L. & John T. Carmody. *Mysticism: Holiness east and west.* Oxford: Oxford University Press, 1996.

Happold, F.C. *Mysticism: A study and an anthology.* London, England: Penguin, 1963.

Horne, *James. Beyond Mysticism* (1978). The moral mystic (1983).

Huegel, F. von. *The mystical element of religion.* 2 vols., London: Dent, 1908; New York: Dutton, 1923.

Katz, Steven, ed. *Mysticism and language* (1992). London and New York: Oxford University Press.

Katz, Steven, ed. *Mysticism and philosophical analysis* (1978). London and New York: Oxford University Press.

Katz, Steven, ed. *Mysticism and religious traditions* (1983). London and New York: Oxford University Press.

McGinn, Bernard. *The foundations of mysticism.* New York: Crossroad Press, 1991.

Otto, Rudolf. *The idea of the holy.* London: Oxford University Press, 1958.

Scholem, Gershom. *Kabbalah.* New York: Dorset Books, 1974.

Scholem, Gershom. *Major trends in Jewish mysticism.* New York: Schocken Books, 1961. (First published in 1941.)

Staal, Frits. *Exploring mysticism.* London, England: Penguin, 1975.

Stace, W. T. *Mysticism and philosophy.* Philadelphia: J. B. Lippencott, 1960.

Underhill, Evelyn. *Mysticism,* 12th edition. New York: Meridian Books, 1955.

Underhill, Evelyn. *Practical mysticism.* New York: E. P. Dutton, 1915.

Weeks, Andrew. *German mysticism. Albany,* New York: SUNY Press, 1993.

Woods, Richard, ed. *Understanding mysticism.* New York: Image Books, 1980.

Zaehner, R.C. *Mysticism: Sacred and profane.* London: Oxford, 1961.

5

Nature Mystics and Mysticism

First, it is pertinent to note that Vaughan and Wordsworth stand pre-eminent among the English poets in being almost exclusively occupied with one theme, the mystical interpretation of nature. Both poets are of a meditative, brooding cast of mind; but whereas Wordsworth arrives at his philosophy entirely through personal experience and sensation, Vaughan is more of a mystical philosopher, deeply read in Plato and the mediæval alchemists. The constant comparison of natural with spiritual processes is, on the whole, the most marked feature of Vaughan's poetry. If man will but attend, he seems to say to us, everything will discourse to him of the spirit. He broods on the silk-worm's change into the butterfly (*Resurrection and Immortality*); he ponders over the mystery of the continuity of life as seen in the plant, dying down and entirely disappearing in winter, and shooting up anew in the spring (*The Hidden Flower*); or, while wandering by his beloved river Usk, he meditates near the deep pool of a waterfall on its mystical significance as it seems to linger beneath the banks and then to shoot onward in swifter course, and he sees in it an image of life beyond the grave.

The seed growing secretly in the earth suggests to him the growth of the soul in the darkness of physical matter; and in *Affliction* he points out that all nature is governed by a law of periodicity and contrast, night and day, sunshine and shower; and as the beauty of colour can only exist by contrast, so are pain, sickness, and trouble needful for the development of man. These poems are sufficient to illustrate the temper of Vaughan's mind, his keen, reverent observation of nature in all her moods, and his intense interest in the minutest happenings, because they are all manifestations of the one mighty law. Vaughan appears to have had a more definite belief in pre-existence than Wordsworth, for he refers to it more than once; and *The Retreate*, which is probably the best known of all his poems and must have furnished some suggestion for the *Immortality Ode*, is based upon it.

Vaughan has occasionally an almost perfect felicity of mystical expression, a power he shares with Donne, Keats, Rossetti, and Wordsworth. His ideas then produce their effect through the medium of art, directly on the feelings. The poem called *Quickness* is perhaps the best example of this peculiar quality, which cannot be analysed but must simply be felt; or *The World*, with its magnificent symbol in the opening lines:—

I saw Eternity the other night,
Like a great *Ring* of pure and endless light,
All calm, as it was bright;
And round beneath it, Time, in hours, days, years,
Driv'n by the spheres,
Like a vast shadow mov'd.

It is remarkable that Mysticism is the most salient feature of Wordsworth's poetry, for he was one who saw, whose inward eye was focussed to visions scarce dreamt of by men. It is because of the strangeness and unfamiliarity of his vision that he is a difficult poet to understand, and the key to the understanding of him is a mystic one. People talk of the difficulty of Browning, but he is easy reading compared with a great deal of Wordsworth.

It is just the apparent simplicity of Wordsworth's thought which is so misleading. A statement about him of the following kind would be fairly generally accepted as the truth. Wordsworth was a simple-minded poet with a passion for nature, he found great joy and consolation in the contemplation of the beauty of hills and dales and clouds and flowers, and urged others to find this too; he lived, and recommended others to live a quiet retired unexciting kind of life, and he preached a doctrine of simplicity and austerity. Now, except that Wordsworth had a passion for Nature, there is not a single true statement here.

Wordsworth was not only a poet, he was also a seer, a mystic and a practical psychologist with an amazingly subtle mind, and an unusual capacity for feeling; he lived a life of excitement and passion, and he preached a doctrine of magnificence and glory. It was not the beauty of Nature which brought him joy and peace, but the *life* in Nature. He himself had caught a vision of that life, he knew it and felt it, and it transformed the whole of existence for him. He believed that every man could attain this vision which he so fully possessed, and his whole life's work took the form of a minute and careful analysis of the processes of feeling in his own nature, which he left as a guide for those who would tread the same path. It would be correct to say that the whole of his poetry is a series of notes and investigations devoted to the practical and detailed explanation of how he considered this state of vision might be reached. He disdained no experience—however trivial, apparently—the working of the mind of a peasant child or an idiot boy, the effect produced on his own emotions by a flower, a glowworm, a bird's note, a girl's song; he passed by nothing which might help to throw light on this problem. The experience which Wordsworth was so anxious others should share was the following.

He found that when his mind was freed from pre-occupation with disturbing objects, petty cares, "little enmities and low desires," that he could then reach a condition of equilibrium, which he describes as a "wise passiveness," or a "happy stillness of the mind." He believed this condition could be deliberately induced by a kind of relaxation of the will, and by a stilling of the busy intellect and striving desires. It is a purifying process, an emptying out of all that is worrying, self-assertive, and self-seeking. If we can habitually train ourselves and attune our minds to this condition, we may at any moment come across something which will arouse our emotions, and it is then, when our emotions—thus purified—are excited to the point of passion, that our vision becomes sufficiently clear to enable us to gain actual experience of the "central peace subsisting for ever at the heart of endless agitation." Once seen, this vision changes for us the whole of life; it reveals unity in what to our every-day sight appears to be diversity, harmony where ordinarily we hear but discord, and joy, overmastering joy, instead of sorrow. It is a kind of illumination, whereby in a lightning flash we see that the world is quite different from what it ordinarily appears to be, and when it is over—for the experience is but momentary—it is impossible to describe the vision in precise terms, but the effect of it is such as to inspire and guide the whole subsequent life of the seer. Wordsworth several times depicts this "bliss ineffable" when "all his thought were steeped in feeling."

The well-known passage in *Tintern Abbey* already quoted (p. 7) is one of the finest analysis of it left us by any of the seers, and it closely resembles the accounts given by Plotinus and Boehme of similar experiences.

To Wordsworth this vision came through Nature, and for this reason. He believed that all we see round us is alive, beating with the same life which pulsates in us. It is, he says,—

> my faith that every flower
> Enjoys the air it breathes.

and that if we will but listen and look, we will hear and see and feel this central life. This is the pith of the message we find repeated again and again in various forms throughout

Wordsworth's poetry, and perhaps best summed up at the end of the fourth book of the *Excursion*, a book which should be closely studied by any one who would explore the secret of the poet's outlook upon life. He tells us in the *Prelude* (Book iii.) that even in boyhood it was by this feeling he "mounted to community with highest truth"—

> To every natural form, rock, fruits, or flower,
> Even the loose stones that cover the highway,
> I gave a moral life: I saw them feel,
> Or linked them to some feeling: the great mass
> Lay bedded in a quickening soul, and all
> That I beheld respired with inward meaning.

In brief, Wordsworth, was haunted by the belief that the secret of the universe is written clearly all round us, could we but train and purify our mind and emotions so as to behold it. He believed that we are in something the same attitude towards Nature as an illiterate untrained person might be in the presence of a book containing the philosophy of Hegel. To the educated trained thinker, who by long and arduous discipline has developed his mental powers, that book contains the revelation of the thought of a great mind; whereas to the uneducated person it is merely a bundle of paper with words printed on it.

He can handle it, touch it, see it, he can read the words, he can even understand many of them separately, but the essence of the book and its meaning remains closed to him until he can effect some alteration in himself which will enable him to understand it. Wordsworth's claim is that he had discovered by his own experience a way to effect the necessary alteration in ourselves which will enable us to catch glimpses of the truths expressing themselves all round us. It is a great claim, but he would seem to have justified it.

It is interesting that the steps in the ladder of perfection, as described by Wordsworth, are precisely analogous to the threefold path or "way" of the religious and philosophic mystic, an ethical system or rule of life, of which, very probably, Wordsworth had never heard. The mystic vision was not attained by him, any more than by others, without deliberate renunciation. He lays great stress upon this; and yet it is a point in his teaching sometimes overlooked. He insists repeatedly upon the fact that before any one can taste of these joys of the spirit, he must be purified, disciplined, self-controlled. He leaves us a full account of his purgative stage. Although he started life with a naturally pure and austere temperament, yet he had deliberately to crush out certain strong passions to which he was liable, as well as all personal ambition, all love of power, all desire for fame or money; and to confine himself to the contemplation of such objects as—

> excite
> No morbid passions, no disquietude,
> No vengeance and no hatred.

Remarkably, the *Recluse* he records how he deliberately fought, and bent to other uses, a certain wild passionate delight he felt in danger, a struggle or victory over a foe, in short, some of the primitive instincts of a strong, healthy animal, feelings which few would regard as reprehensible. These natural instincts, this force and energy, good in themselves, Wordsworth did not crush, but deliberately turned into a higher channel.

At the end of the *Prelude* he makes his confession of the sins he did not commit.

> Never did I, in quest of right and wrong,
> Tamper with conscience from a private aim;
> Nor was in any public hope the dupe
> Of selfish passions; nor did ever yield
> Wilfully to mean cares or low pursuits.

Such a confession, or rather boast, in the mouth of

almost any other man would sound hypocritical or self-complacent; but with Wordsworth, we feel it is the bare truth told us for our help and guidance, as being the necessary and preliminary step. It is a high standard which is held up before us, even in this first stage, for it includes, not merely the avoidance of all obvious sins against man and society, but a tuning-up, a transmuting of the whole nature to high and noble endeavour. Wordsworth found his reward, in a settled state of calm serenity, "consummate happiness," "wide-spreading, steady, calm, contemplative," and, as he tells us in the fourth book of the *Prelude*, on one evening during that summer vacation,

> Gently did my soul
> Put off her veil, and, self-transmuted, stood
> Naked, as in the presence of her God.

It is significant to note that when the mind and soul have been prepared, the next step is concentration, aspiration. Then it is borne in upon the poet that in the infinite and in the eternal alone can we find rest, can we find ourselves; and towards this infinitude we must strive with unflagging ardour;

> Our destiny, our being's heart and home,
> Is with infinitude, and only there.
> *Prelude*, Book vi. 604.

Remarkably, the result of this aspiration towards the infinite is a quickening of consciousness, upon which follows the attainment of the third or unitive stage, the moment when man can "breathe in worlds to which the heaven of heavens is but a veil," and perceive "the forms whose kingdom is where time and place are not."

Such minds—

> need not extraordinary calls
> To rouse them; in a world of life they live,

By sensible impressions not enthralled,
... the highest bliss
That flesh can know *is theirs*—the consciousness
Of Whom they are.
Prelude, Book xiv. 105, 113,

Wordsworth possessed in a peculiar degree a mystic sense of infinity, of the boundless, of the opening-out of the world of our normal finite experience into the transcendental; and he had a rare power of putting this into words. It was a feeling which, as he tells us in the *Prelude* (Book xiii.), he had from earliest childhood, when the disappearing line of the public highway—

Was like an invitation into space
Boundless, or guide into eternity,

a feeling which, applied to man, gives that inspiriting certitude of boundless growth, when the soul has—

... an obscure sense
Of possible sublimity, whereto
With growing faculties she doth aspire.

It is at this point, and on this subject, that Wordsworth's poetical and ethical imagination are most nearly fused. This fusion is far from constant with him; and the result is that there are tracts of his writings where the sentiments are excellent, the philosophy illuminating, but the poetry is not great: it does not awaken the "transcendental feeling." The moments when this condition is most fully attained by Wordsworth occur when, by sheer force of poetic imagination combined with spiritual insight, in some mysterious and indescribable way, he flashes upon us a sensation of boundless infinity.

Herein consists the peculiar magic of such a poem as *Stepping Westward*; and there is a touch of the same feeling in the *Solitary Reaper*. It is hardly necessary to dwell on other mystical elements in Wordsworth, such as his belief in the one law governing all things, "from creeping plant to sovereign man," and the hint of belief in pre-existence in the *Ode on Immortality*. His attitude towards life as a whole is to be found in a few lines in the "after-thought" to the Duddon sonnets.

> The Form remains, the Function never dies;
> While we, the brave, the mighty and the wise,
> We Men, who in our morn of youth defied
> The elements, must vanish:—be it so!
> Enough, if something from our hands have power
> To live, and act, and serve the future hour;
> And if, as toward the silent tomb we go,
> Through love, through hope, and faith's transcendent dower,
> We feel that we are greater than we know.

In fact, Richard Jefferies is closely akin to Wordsworth in his overpowering consciousness of the life in nature. This consciousness is the strongest force in him, so that at times he is almost submerged by it, and he loses the sense of outward things. In this condition of trance the sense of time vanishes, there is, he asserts, no such thing, no past or future, only now, which is eternity.

In *The Story of My Heart*, a rhapsody of mystic experience and aspiration he describes in detail several such moments of exaltation or trance. He seems to be peculiarly sensitive to sunshine. As the moon typifies to Keats the eternal essence in all things, so to Jefferies the sun seems to be the physical expression or symbol of the central Force of the world, and it is through gazing on sunlight that he most often enters into the trance state. Standing, one summer's morning, in a recess on London Bridge, he looks out on the sunshine "burning on steadfast," "lighting the great heaven; gleaming on my finger-nail."

"I was intensely conscious of it," he writes, "I felt it; I felt the presence of the immense powers of the universe; I felt out into the depths of the ether. So intensely conscious of the sun, the sky, the limitless space, I felt too in the midst of eternity then, in the midst of the supernatural, among the immortal, and the greatness of the material realised the spirit. By these I saw my soul; by these I knew the supernatural to be more intensely real than the sun. I touched the supernatural, the immortal, there that moment."

When he reaches this state, outer things drop away, and he seems to become lost, and absorbed into the being of the universe. He partakes, momentarily, of a larger, fuller life, he drinks in vitality through nature. The least blade of grass, he says, or the greatest oak, "seemed like exterior nerves and veins for the conveyance of feeling to me. Sometimes a very ecstasy of exquisite enjoyment of the entire visible universe filled me."

This great central Life Force, which Jefferies, like Wordsworth, seemed at moments to touch, he, in marked contrast to other mystics, refuses to call God. For, he says, what we understand by deity is the purest form of mind, and he sees no mind in nature. It is a force without a mind, "more subtle than electricity, but absolutely devoid of consciousness and with no more feeling than the force which lifts the tides."

Yet this cannot content him, for later he declares there must be an existence higher than deity, towards which he aspires and presses with the whole force of his being. "Give me," he cries, "to live the deepest soul-life now and always with this 'Highest Soul.'" This thrilling consciousness of spiritual life felt through nature, coupled with passionate aspiration to be absorbed in that larger life, are the two main features of the mysticism of Richard Jefferies. His books, and especially *The Story of My Heart*, contain, together with the most exquisite nature description, a rich and vivid record of sensation, feeling, and aspiration. But it is a feeling which, though vivifying, can only be expressed in general terms, and it carries with it no vision and no philosophy. It is almost entirely emotional, and it is as an emotional record that it is of value, for Jefferies' intellectual reflections are, for the most part, curiously contradictory and unconvincing.

The certainty and rapture of this experience of spiritual emotion is all the more amazing when we remember that the record of it was written in agony, when he was wrecked with mortal illness and his nerves were shattered with pain. For with him, as later with Francis Thompson, physical pain and material trouble seemed to serve only to direct him towards and to enhance the glory of the spiritual vision.

After having an understanding of `nature mystics', now we will put light on nature mysticism'.

NATURE MYSTICISM

Here it is worth mentioning that American nature writer, Joseph Wood Krutch, has insisted that caring about nature is mystical in origin; and Arne Naess, an influential Norwegian philosopher, who champions nature for nature's sake, once spoke of a compelling emotional experience that seems to be the driving force for passionate environmentalism. It is the experience many people have in nature of being connected to something greater than their ego — it is a sort of oceanic feeling. This mystical experience is the burning bush, which gives champions of wilderness and animal rights a sense of mission, rightness and purpose.

In *The Gentle Art of Tramping*, Stephen Graham said, "As you sit on the hillside, or lie prone under the trees of the forest, or sprawl wet-legged by a mountain stream, the great door, that does not look like a door, opens." Annie Dillard, writing about her solitary nature experiences in the southern Appalachians, said this: "Experiencing the present purely is being empty and hollow; you catch grace as a man fills his cup under a waterfall". She wrote of a nature experience where she felt like an immense bell that was being struck. In a letter to his brother, Theo, Van Gogh once confessed that he had "a terrible need of—shall I say the word—religion. Then I go out and paint the stars." Christianity's greatest mystic, Meister Eckhart, spoke of the sublime moment when "all blades of grass, wood, and stone, all things are One." The mythologist, Joseph Campbell, once said God is the experience of looking at a tree and saying, "Ah!"

The *Centuries of Meditations* of Thomas Traherne, written in the seventeenth century, but not published until the early twen tieth century, rhapsodized about the divine presence in the beauties of the earth. "You never enjoy the world aright," he wrote, "'till the sea itself floweth in your veins, 'till you are clothed with the heavens and crowned with the stars."

Charlene Spretnak wrote the following:

> There are sacred moments in life when we experience in rational and very direct ways that separation, the boundary between ourselves and other people and between ourselves and Nature, is illusion. Oneness is reality. We can experience that stasis is illusory and that reality is continual flux and change on very subtle and also on gross levels of perception . .

She says a prime way for experiencing these sublime moments is to go into wilderness, approaching it with silence and alertness, while carefully observing the flow of inner and outer events.

Anyone who does this, she says, will eventually come to perceive "a deep, deep silence and a oneness that is almost palpable." Spretnak says at such moments the distinction between inner and outer mind dissipates.

The mystical feeling in nature is most often described as a feeling of oneness.

Rousseau wrote this about his experiences on Peter Island on the Lake of Bienne:

> "As evening approached, I came down from the heights of the island, and I liked then to go and sit on the shingle in some secluded spot by the lake; there the noise of the waves and the movement of the water, taking hold of my senses and driving all other agitation from my soul, would plunge me into delicious reverie in which night often stole upon me unawares."

The words of Byron express the oneness with nature, which has, since Rousseau, been the obsession of nature mystics: "I live not in myself, but I became a portion of all around me, and to me high mountains are a feeling . . ." Byron also wrote: "Are not the mountains, waves and skies a part of me and of my soul, as I of them?"

Nature mysticism often sounds like pantheism. Consider these fragments from a poem by the Asian poet, Rumi:

> I am the dust in the sunlight, I am the ball of the sun . . .
> I am the mist of morning, the breath of evening . . . .
> I am the spark in the stone, the gleam of gold in the metal . . . .
> The rose and the nightingale drunk with its fragrance.
> I am the chain of being, the circle of the spheres,
> The scale of creation, the rise and the fall.
> I am what is and is not . . .
> I am the soul in all.

In her book called *Ecstasy*, Laski reports research findings indicating that the most frequent trigger for mystical experi ences is nature, with nature art being the second most frequent trigger. Another national survey found that almost half of all the people who have had mystical experiences consider the beauties of nature to be the primary inspiration.

Rudolf Otto defined nature mysticism as "the sense of being immersed in the oneness of nature, so that man feels all the individuality, all the peculiarities of natural things in himself. He dances with the motes of dust and radiates with the sun; he rises with the dawn, surges with the wave, is fragrant with the rose, rapt with the nightingale: he knows and is all being, all strength, all joy, all desire, all pain in all things inseparably." Aldous Huxley called mystical oneness with nature "the perennial philosophy".

Stace suggested that mystical experiences can be classified as either extraverted or introverted. In introverted mysticism, the environment is lost. This occurs to those who, like St. Augustine, reject the sensuousness of natural phenomena and enter into a world of pure spirit. Augustine believed we should aban don the world and its beauty. The beauties of nature, he believed, are vain and transitory. To love nature is to become a slave to nature and to turn away from spiritual abstractions which are embedded in the eternal.

It is the second type, extraverted mysticism, which is a nature experience. In extraverted mysticism, the surroundings are "lit up" and the world appears to us as it did in all its numinous glory to Adam on the day of creation. A good example of extraverted mysticism is in the verse of Kabir, a fifteenth century poet from India, which Robert Bly has translated and paraphrased:

> Friend, hope for the Guest while you are alive . . . .
> If you do not break your ropes while you're alive,
> do you think
> Ghosts will do it after?

Aldous Huxley aided by mescaline said, "I was seeing

what Adam had seen on the morning of creation — the miracle, moment by moment of naked existence." Gazing at flowers he reported experiencing "a transcendence that was yet eternal life, a per petual perishing that was at the same time pure Being, a bundle of minute, unique particulars in which, by some unspeakable and yet self-evident paradox was to be seen the divine source of all existence." Meister Eckhart spoke of this Adamic seeing when he wrote, "If you want to discover nature's nakedness, you must destroy its symbols."

Some Freudian psychologists have equateded the "oneness" feeling in nature and religion with regressive fantasies of being one with one's Mother. We were one with her in the womb, and as infants we experienced oneness at her breast. Jung, in *Symbols of Transformation*, carefully described how the imagery of nature mysticism tends to use maternal symbols.

Nature mysticism can be — but is not necessarily — experienced as a sense of being in the presence of the divine. Seneca wrote: "When you enter a grove peopled with ancient trees, higher than the ordinary, and shutting out the sky with their thickly inter-twined branches, do not the stately shadows of the wood, the stillness of the place, and the awful gloom of this doomed cavern then strike you with the presence of a deity?"

There is something about woodlands, mountains and deserts that evokes awe and religious sentiments. Large stands of ancient trees give us a sense of the vast, the holy, the unspeakable. We sense being a part of something far larger than our individual egos and feel connected to eternity. In the Celtic iron age the Druids worshiped in sacred oak-groves. Novelist, John Fowles once said all sacred places derive their aura from forest settings.

English writer and nature lover W. H. Hudson wrote in *The Purple Land* :

For here the religion that languishes in crowded cities or steals shame-faced to hide itself in dim churches, flourishes greatly, filling the soul with a solemn joy. Face to face with Nature on the vast hills at eventide, who does not feel himself near to the Unseen?

According to historian, Arnold Toynbee, the relationship between religion and nature is an irreducible fact.

Western Religious Tradition

In his *Confessions*, St. Augustine told of his attempts to seek God in the world of Nature, but argues that it was a mistake or it leads one to concentrate on the wrong things: "Not us, not us," he insisted, "but Him who made us." Augustine's words did not stop other Christian mystic from attempting to seek God through nature. Meister Eckhart spoke of the experience when "all blades of grass, wood, and stone, all things are One." [repeat] Jacob Boehme wrote, "In this light, my spirit saw through all things and into all creatures, and I recognized God in grass and plants." Gregory of Nyssa wrote, "Traveling through the creation, the virtuous man is led to the apprehension of the Master of the Creation." And Suso wrote, "O tender God, if Thou art so living in Thy creatures, how fair and lovely must Thou be in Thyself." *Francis of Asissi* considered all created things—birds, beasts, flowers, sun, moon, even death—to be children of God and his brothers and sisters in Christ. John Smith wrote, "There is a twofold meaning in every creature, a literal and a mystical, and the one is but the ground of the other."

Non-Western Religious Tradition

Nature mysticism is also prevalent in the literature of the East. A Zen Buddhist monk asks, for example, "How may I enter in the Way?" His master points to a mountain steam and says, "Do you hear the murmur of the stream? There you may enter." The *Zenrinkushu* says the lines of the hills are the Pure Body of Buddha. There is an ancient

Zen saying that the mountains, the rivers, the earth, everything that happens, is — without exception — your own mind. Dogon, a Zen masater who lived from 1200 to 1253 a.d.spoke of mountains and rivers as being an immediate and direct revelation of truth; he said they are perfect exactly as they are: "Mountains and rivers at this very moment are the actualization of the world of the ancient Buddhas. Each, abiding in its phenomenal expression, realizes completeness."

6

20th Century Nature Mysticism

Here in this chapter we intend to attempt an investigation of what a 'nature mysticism' might be as indicated primarily by four writers: Traherne, Whitman, Jefferies, and Krishnamurti. These have been chosen because their writings are substantially mystical or at least because their mysticism is more easily identified than with others such as Wordsworth and a whole range of other writers and poets through the ages. These other sources are vital to a fuller development of this subject but time does not permit the much longer trawl through these less populated 'seas'.

Any writer on mysticism will inevitably bring certain assumptions with them to the subject, so it is important to state these at the outset. While broadly sympathetic to the definitions of mysticism given by James, Underhill, Zaehner and Happold, I am generally interested in a mysticism that does not require either the religious, the paranormal, or the occult. Hence no great effort will be expended to justify the concept of a nature mysticism against the very real (to them) worries that an orthodox Christian might have; nor on the other hand will it readily be ceded that nature mysticism might expand to include Blake's or Steiner's angels or any other occult or supernatural phenomenon. I also have to state that I accept the perennialist view (popularised by Huxley) as against the contextual view (promoted by Katz et. al.). The perennialist view holds that at core we are looking at one phenomenon called mysticism as against many, so that any taxonomy of mysticism is more a taxonomy of paths than of ends. On the other hand the traditionalist view (epitomised by the works of Frithjof Schuon) is not useful here as it assumes that any 'real' experience of God has to come via established religion, so it would neither accept the importance of Traherne, Whitman, Jefferies, or Krishnamurti, or even the concept of nature mysticism.

Another important caveat on a too-ready acceptance of the above scholars' definitions of mysticism is that their definitions are perhaps too bound up with mystical *experience*. Although a discussion of discrete experiences, usually understood to be in some way 'peak' experiences, is useful, it obscures the fact that the lives of the mystics need also to be characterised in terms of their continuum or orientation.

As a rough working definition to begin the discussion of nature mysticism we can say that it is an expansivity triggered by Nature. This expansivity will include not only discrete experiences (such as certain raptures often cited as examples of nature mysticism) but a mystical continuum or orientation in which Nature plays a role.

Via Positiva and Via Negativa

Although the place of nature mysticism in existing taxonomies of mysticism will be explored later on, it is worth introducing at this point the distinction, widely held to be useful, between *via positiva* and *via negativa*. *Via negativa* is the more easily defined of the two: it is the path to mystical union via the denying of all manifest things. The work of Dyonisius the Areopagite is perhaps the best example in a Western context, but the same principles are found as far afield as in branches of Hinduism ('neti, neti' meaning 'not this, not that' is its Indian formulation); in Buddhism (in the very concept of *nirvana* or nothingness); and in modern sages like Krishnamurti and Douglas Harding. *Via negativa* carries with it associations of withdrawal, solitude, contemplation, silence, simplicity, and renunciation, though these are often caricatured, as in the supposed Christian 'heresy' of quietism.

Via positiva is the path of expansion, a growing capacity to lose boundaries and temporality until one becomes the Whole. Perhaps the best exponent of this path is Whitman. One might more readily recognise *via positiva* in an ecstatic like Rumi or Kabir. Clearly nature mysticism will be more readily associated with *via positiva* than *via negativa*, but it does not in the least require one aspect common in *via positiva*: the devotional orientation, or at least not a theistic devotion.

The distinction between *via positiva* and *via negativa* is a difficult one, and even more so the relationship between this distinction and those between *bhakti* and *jnani*, heart and intellect, love and awareness, and theistic and monistic mysticism, and so on. All of these are useful signposts however.

The Role of Nature in Mysticism

If nature mysticism is perhaps more closely related to *via positiva* however, then what is the role of Nature in this form of mysticism? Some pointers as to what we are looking for are needed here. We have mentioned that Nature might be a trigger, that is a trigger to a discrete mystical experience, and that it might also be part of the continuum or orientation of a mystic. We can easily investigate the first case, as there are many recorded accounts of mystical experiences that took place as a result of the contemplation of a mountain, sunset, or even of humbler commonplace Nature: these are ecstatic or sublime moments. How can we learn about Nature as part of the continuum of the mystic however?

The answer may lie in a simple characterisation of a mystic's writings: they may pedagogical, or they may be the spontaneous celebration of the delight they find in their condition. This distinction is very important because the pedagogical is more often a picture of the mystic's audience than of their inner world for some such as Krishnamurti there is no allowance made for the listener, while for others such as Gurdjieff it is almost impossible to disentangle pedagogical device from the real teaching. Hence to understand the role of Nature in the continuum of the mystic can take some detective work.

Nature as a trigger to mystical experience can be understood, as identified earlier, as part of an expansivity. It may also cause the resonance of some faculty that goes beyond time, so that as a *cause* of the loss of boundaries and as a *cause* of the loss of the sense of time Nature somehow works on certain individuals. Nature is vast, though this is often lost on city dwellers, and it is timeless in the sense that it regenerates itself. It is also *prodigious*, and this is part of *via positiva*: Arjuna's overwhelming experience of the cosmic nature of Krishna in the *Bhagavad Gita* is partly due to the abundance of creation that is manifest through Krishna. The views of Nature that we shall come across in nature mysticism are not romanticised views of Nature however, even if they may seem so on the surface. Nature can also be seen as the destroyer of the false, and this is important in Buddhist mysticism for example the Buddha nature is revealed once the imperfections of vision are removed, rather than by grace as in the Christian tradition.

Scholars on Nature Mysticism

Recent debates amongst scholars of mysticism have focused on the perennialist / contextualist argument in which nature mysticism plays no important role. Hence it is more useful to look back at earlier scholars like Bucke, James, and Underhill who provided much of the basis at the turn of the century for later work; we also look at the work of an obscure author, J. Edward Mercer, and R.C. Zaehner, who wrote on nature mysticism in connection with drugs.

William James

In the *Varieties of Religious Experience* William James introduced an influential distinction between the religion of the healthy-minded and that of the sick soul, locating nature mysticism (without an emphasis on it by name however) in the healthy-minded. The distinction is useful because it helps focus on the problems of evil and innocence, both of which are inextricably linked with nature mysticism. James was unaware of the work of Jefferies or Traherne, but he knew of Whitman and in a way that is not well understood today. At the end of the nineteenth century 'Whitmanism' as a proto-religion was much discussed; it is only more recently that Whitman studies has become merely literary, and James was reacting to the earlier debates. James makes this comment on Whitman:

> "In some individuals optimism may become quasi-pathological. The capacity for even a transitory sadness or a momentary humility seems cut off from them as by a kind of congenital anaesthesia. The supreme contemporary example of such an inability to feel evil is of course Walt Whitman. "

This grossly misrepresents Whitman as we shall see later. James continues:

> Thus it has come about that many persons to-day regard Walt Whitman as the restorer of the eternal natural religion. He has infected them with his own love of comrades, with his own gladness that he and they exist. Societies are actually formed for his cult; a periodical organ exists for its propagation, in which the lines of orthodoxy and heterodoxy are already beginning to be drawn; hymns are written by others in his peculiar prosody; and he is even explicitly compared to the founder of the Christian religion, not altogether to the advantage of the latter.

Coming back to James's view of Whitman later, but it is interesting to note that he uses the term 'eternal natural religion'. Throughout James's chapter on the healthy-minded he attempts an even-handedness but we can see that his instinct is with the religion of the sick soul. I believe that James taps into a universal interest in evil, the morbid, and the penitent; this interest makes *via negativa* such a strong current in mysticism. Nature mysticism should not be assumed to require the naive healthy-mindedness of James however. In his chapter on the sick soul James puts forward ('without judgement' he tells us) the view that 'naturism' is pessimistic because 'Old age has the last word: the purely naturalistic look at life, however enthusiastically it may begin, is sure to end in sadness.' (Modern adherents to this view gleefully cite the case of Whitman in his old age as an example.) 'Naturism' in this context is far removed from the concerns of nature mysticism. James underpins his healthy/sick dichotomy with a further distinction: between the once-born and twice-born the former are permanently in an innocent state of happiness and the latter regain it through some form of salvation. This forms the basis of two types of religion for him: naturalism and salvationism, and we shall consider this view in the nature mysticism of Traherne, Whitman and Jefferies. Before leaving James it is useful to comment on another important contribution he made to the study of mysticism: his four 'marks' of mystical experience.

These are: ineffability, noetic quality, transiency and passivity. These marks have been largely adopted by later writers on mysticism, and perhaps have set the trend to consider mystical experience at the expense of mystical orientation. James concludes on the general traits of the mystic range of consciousness:

> It is on the whole pantheistic and optimistic, or at least the opposite of pessimistic. It is anti-naturalistic, and harmonizes best with twice-bornness and so-called other-worldly states of mind.

James's dismissal of Whitman, his obvious preference for the sick soul, and his emphasis on mystical experience do not diminish however his contribution to the study of mysticism, in particular his recognition of the authority that mystical experience brings to the experiencer.

Evelyn Underhill

Evelyn Underhill first published her *Mysticism The Nature and Development of Spiritual Consciousness* in 1911, some nine years after James' *Varieties*. It built on the work of James and Bucke (who also influenced James); it focused on mysticism; it was broader in its sources, though it did not venture further than the Religions of the Book (considering mystics of the Far East to be nihilists); and it shared the emphasis on mystical experience (adding further 'marks' to James' scheme). Of the four main protagonists in this essay Underhill was aware of Whitman and Jefferies, neither of whom she acknowledged as full-blown mystics. Unlike James she placed no great emphasis on the distinction between the healthy-minded and the sick soul, seeing in the mystics a universal earnestness and determination in their pursuit of the absolute. There are many sympathetic references to Nature none of which make the association with naive healthy-mindedness that James implies. Here are some examples:

> Such use of visible nature as the stuff of ontological perceptions, the medium whereby the self reaches out to the Absolute, is not rare in the history of mysticism. The mysterious vitality of trees, the silent magic of the forest, the strange and steady cycle of its life, possess in a peculiar degree this power of unleashing the human soul: are curiously friendly to its cravings, minister to its inarticulate needs. Unsullied by the corroding touch of consciousness, that life can make a contact with the "great life of All"; and through its mighty rhythms man can receive a message concerning the true and timeless World of "all that is, and was, and evermore shall be." Plant life of all kinds, indeed

from the "flower in the crannied wall" to the "Woods of Westermain" can easily become for selves of a certain type, a "mode of the Infinite." So obviously does this appear when we study the history of the mystics, that Steiner has drawn from it the hardly warrantable inference that "plants are just those natural phenomena whose qualities in the higher world are similar to their qualities in the physical world."

Though the conclusion be not convincing, the fact remains. The flowery garment of the world is for some mystics a medium of ineffable perception, a source of exalted joy, the veritable clothing of God. This is hardly to add that such a state of things has always been found incredible by common sense. "The trees which move some to tears of joy," says Blake, who possessed in an eminent degree this form of sacramental perception, "is in the Eyes of others only a green thing that stand in the Way." To "see God in nature," to attain a radiant consciousness of the "otherness" of natural things, is the simplest and commonest form of illumination. Most people, under the spell of emotion or beauty, have known flashes of rudimentary vision of this kind.

Where such a consciousness is recurrent, as it is in may poets, there results that partial yet often overpowering apprehension of the Infinite Life immanent in all living things, which some modern writers have dignified by the name of "nature-mysticism." In the first passage Underhill hints at a personal sensitivity to nature, though in the second one is left with the impression that "nature-mysticism" is for her too grand a term. (I am not sure also whether her dismissal of Steiner is warranted: his theories were not derived from a study of the mystics.) Incidentally, she gives the following as a list of poets that fit the description in the passage: Keats, Shelley, Wordsworth, Tennyson, Browning and Whitman.

Remarkably, Underhill is keen to defend the mystic

from the general assumption that they deny the world; she often uses their relation to Nature to illustrate this. At one point she cites the seeing of "all creatures in God, and God in all creatures"; at another the brother Wolf of Francis of Assisi; and at another the case of the Peruvian Saint, Rose of Lima, who sang the praises of God for a whole hour in alternation with a songbird. In another passage Underhill recommends natural objects as subjects for contemplation. Seen thus a thistle has celestial qualities: a speckled hen a touch of the sublime. Our greater comrades, the trees, the clouds, the rivers, initiate us into mighty secrets, flame out at us "like shining from shook foil." The "eye which looks upon Eternity" has been given its opportunity. We have been immersed for a moment in the "life of the All": a deep and peaceful love unites us with the substance of all things, a "Mystic Marriage" has taken place between the mind and some aspect of the external world. *Cor ad cor loquitur*: Life has spoken to life, but not only to the surface-intelligence. That surface-intelligence knows only that the message was true and beautiful: no more.

The price of this experience has been a stilling of that surface-mind, a calling in of all our scattered interests: an entire giving of ourselves to this one activity, without self-consciousness, without reflective thought. To reflect is always to distort: our minds are not good mirrors. The contemplative, on whatever level his faculty may operate, is contented to absorb and be absorbed: and by this humble access he attains to a plane of knowledge which no intellectual process can come near.

In fact, this simple experiment is in any sense to be equated with the transcendental contemplation of the mystic. Yet it exercises on a small scale, and in regard to visible Nature, the same natural faculties which are taken up and used it is true upon other levels, and in subjection to the transcendental sense in his apprehension of the Invisible Real. Though it is one thing to see truthfully for an instant the flower in the crannied wall, another to be lifted up to the apprehension of "eternal Truth, true Love and loved Eternity", yet both according to their measure are functions of the inward eye, operating in the "suspension of the mind."

Underhill leaves us with many question regarding a possible nature mysticism in this passage, the principle one being whether it really is a lesser mysticism, any more than 'quietism' is really to be treated as deficient. There are also useful pointers in this passage regarding the silence of the mind in which Nature speaks to us.

Edward Mercer

Mercer was aware of Jefferies and Whitman (both of whom are quoted extensively, though Jefferies more so) but not of Traherne or Krishnamurti; he does also cite James' *Varieties*. *Nature Mysticism* is scholarly review of a wide range of sources, stating at the same time that 'metaphysics and theology are to be avoided' the latter surprising as Mercer was bishop of Tasmania. He gives us a useful definition of nature mysticism that can complement the first approximation given earlier:

> "The goal of the nature-mystics is actual living communion with the Real, in and through its sensuous manifestation."

This definition is useful because it avoids the emphasis on ecstatic or otherwise special experiences and focuses more on a continuum, as implied in the word communion. The use of the term 'the Real,' though vague at this point, is also useful if we place it for the time being merely in opposition to the false or fanciful (thus alerting us to the danger of the romantic or merely aesthetic dimension of nature mysticism). Mercer is careful also to deal with the charge of anthropomorphism and also deals with the issue of animism (quoting Wordsworth's recollection of a boyhood incident on a lake where a peak seems to come alive to him).

Mercer is oddly cautious about nature itself, spending many chapters on the elements (eight on water, two on air, and one on fire) before dealing briefly with vegetation; he more or less rules out a discussion of animal life. Despite this the book is valuable, particularly for its conviction that nature mysticism is worthwhile in itself and also for the view that its pursuance can be fostered.

Zaehner

Richard Charles Zaehner wrote and translated prodigiously in religion and mysticism and expanded on the works of Bucke, James, and Underhill by his scholarship in Eastern mysticism (he does not seem to be aware of Mercer's work). Compared to these three he is a slippery character however in that his own views as a Catholic are hidden by a two- or three-deep layering of academic scepticism. Like Underhill however he regards nature mysticism, for which he coins the term panenhenic mysticism, as inferior to monistic mysticism, which in turn is inferior to theistic mysticism.

The usefulness of his term panenhenic mysticism is diminished by his association of its domain, nature mysticism, with drug-induced 'mystical' states, particularly in his book *Mysticism, Drugs, and Makebelieve* first published in 1972. Much of this book is a re-presentation of an earlier work called *Mysticism Sacred and Profane*, first published in 1957. Zaehner knew of all four of the major protagonists in this essay, though he seems to reserve an unqualified admiration only for Krishnamurti, referring to him as a 'holy man'. Nature mysticism has 23 entries in the index to *Mysticism, Drugs, and Makebelieve,* and deals at length with the subject in the chapter called 'The Vitalist Heresy.' Zaehner equates nature mysticism with cosmic consciousness (a term introduced by Richard Maurice Bucke, but who is dismissed by Zaehner as 'fatuous') and says of it that 'is essential to most of the experiences described in the Hindu sacred books.' He points out that for Proust as for many other nature mystics a mystical experience may come unheralded, but for Zen students, where a similarly mundane natural object or event might trigger a similar experience, they have been trained to seek it out and recognise it.

Zaehner seems to classify Zen with nature mysticism, and tends to relegate both to an inferior status than other forms. Typical of his mix of cant and scholarly dispassion, he goes on to praise the work of the Irish novelist Forrest Reid as beautifully expressing the experience of the typical nature mystic. Because however drug-induced experiences can induce similar states he goes on to criticise James for not distinguishing nature mysticism clearly enough from the kind of transcendental mysticism of Buddhism. (Incidentally he twice states of James that 'his sympathies were plainly all on the side of the 'healthy-minded' against the 'sick soul' who must be born again' the opposite of my own reading!) At the end of the 'Vitalist Heresy' Zaehner groups Jefferies and Whitman as nature mystics, with Whitman perhaps the most thoroughgoing; he then slips into an attack on the Upanishads as the vitalist heresy (which in typical Zaehner style is meant half-ironically):

> All this had of course been said thousands of years ago in the Upanishads, the fount and origin of all nature mysticism, for here too we find the perfect expression of 'Whitmanism' in all its preposterous defiance of logic and common sense.

However Zaehner's association of nature mysticism with the Upanishads is useful, though it is Taoism that may be a better source for understanding it. He also mentions Spinoza in connection with nature mysticism. Speaking on Timothy Leary's account of the Catholic communion as giving an ecstatic revelation (similar to LSD) Zaehner perhaps sums up his attitude to nature mysticism:

In fact, this is perfectly fair account of Christian mysticism: it is the soul's love-affair with God and its spiritual marriage to him. It is not a merging into the All as so often in the Upanishads or with the nature mystics, nor is it the isolation of one's own eternal essence from all that is other than itself as in the Shankya-Yoga in India. Zaehner is entitled to the opinion that nature mysticism as he characterises it is fundamentally different from Christian mysticism and inferior to it, but Mercer's view, that nature mysticism is valuable regardless of its similarities or otherwise to other forms, is probably the best to take in the long run.

Happold

F.C.Happold's work, called simply *Mysticism*, was first published in 1962. Happold acknowledges it as a personal anthology and commentary, though he builds again on the work of James and Underhill; he takes for example James' four marks of mystical experience and expands them to six by adding a sense of Oneness and a sense of timelessness. Happold does not claim to move forward our understanding of mysticism in any significant way, but does present a more balanced view than Zaehner. He gives equal weight to what he calls nature-, soul- and god-mysticism (corresponding to Zaehner's three categories), and devotes a chapter respectively to Traherne and Jefferies.

Happold shares with the other scholars mentioned here the emphasis on mystical experience; a confirmation of this comes from an account of Happold's visit to the great English mystic Douglas Harding, in which Harding tells of Happold's insistence on hearing about peak mystical experiences instead of Douglas' very down-to-earth teachings. Harding's own description of what comes nearest to a mystical experience is found in the opening chapter of his *On Having No Head*, but, like Krishnamurti he consistently plays down the role of 'peak' experience.

In Religious and Mystical Traditions

A detailed analysis of the role of nature and nature mysticism in Judaism, Christianity, and Islam is beyond the scope of this essay, apart from some general remarks. The Gnostic and Manichean influence on Christian thought has made Nature and the body an area often set in opposition to the spiritual. This may be less so in Judaism and Islam. Christian mystics are generally agreed to have been more cautious in their language than Hindu or Buddhist mystics; Sufi mystics have also run into trouble with mainstream Islam. The theistic nature of Judaism, Christianity and Islam make nature mysticism more difficult to accommodate than in Hinduism or Buddhism.

An interesting example of how a modern Christian might view nature mysticism is that of Anthony Freeman, the Church of England sacked for 'not believing in God.' He writes:

> Emotionally I hung on to the design argument long after conceding that there was no intellectual force in it. And it was my emotional response, to a growing doubt that the universe really has a design, which finally tipped the balance against it. I can still admire the way in which elements of nature interlock, but I can no longer accept that it is part of a plan. For example I can marvel that animals have so developed that they can breath air; I cannot accept (as the old view required) that God made air the way he did in order that the animals could breathe. Nor can I accept any longer (as traditional faith requires) that a good and skilful God would have designed so much waste and violence into nature, 'red in tooth and claw.'

Freeman is proposing a humanist Christianity, but what is interesting here is that in closing the door to a Christian God (at least the one taught in the seminaries) he is also closing the door to a nature mysticism. To see waste and violence in Nature, to see it as 'red in tooth and claw', and not see its beauty, tenderness, and intimations of the infinite and the eternal is to lose out indeed. This pessimism is however a widespread view of Nature, and we need to keep this example in mind as we examine further on the prerequisites for a nature mysticism.

Zaehner rightly points out that the Hindu Upanishads

say much that is consistent with nature mysticism, though it is hard to point to specific passages. What is often found is a regard for the natural order and for Nature in all its aspects, including the sexual. Although this may be hard to demonstrate, one is left with the suspicion that the Hindus of 2 to 3 thousand years ago, authors of the Upanishads, were more accepting of nature than at present; that renunciation has grown from a symbolic act and a simple choice of lifestyle to an active rejection of Nature.

In the lives and teachings of those wonderful sages, Ramakrishna and Ramana Maharshi, we find no pleasure in Nature, and in the life of Gandhi an extreme of renunciation. Of modern Indian-born teachers it is the iconoclast Rajneesh and the Western-educated Krishnamurti who show a sensitivity and appreciation of Nature. Taoism, as the ancestor of Zen, is a more obviously promising ground for the development of a nature mysticism. The Tao Teh Ching is an unusual document in the history of mysticism, and quite unlike any Buddhist text, in that it seems to speak of the post-enlightenment stage in a matter-of-fact way; pointing out that the Tao is likely to be misunderstood; that the sage is like the infant yet rules or guides his or her community; that with the least interference the natural order will prosper; and that the sage prefers what is within to what is without. It is anti-intellectual and anti-technology. Suzuki points this out through a story from Chang-tze:

A farmer dug a well and was using the water for irrigating his farm. He used an ordinary bucket to draw water from the well, as most primitive people do. A passer-by, seeing this, asked the farmer why he did not use a shadoof for the purpose; it is a labour-saving device and can do more work than the primitive method.

The farmer said. "I know it is a labour-saving and it is for this very reason that I do not use the device. What I am afraid of is that the use of such a contrivance makes one machine-minded. Machine-mindedness leads one to the habit of indolence and laziness.

Suzuki considers Orientals more attuned to Nature than Westerners, giving as an example two poems, the first by Basho:

When I look carefully
I see the *nazuna* blooming
By the hedge!

Suzuki explains that he has translated the Japanese word *kana* into the finishing exclamation mark in the poem; it expresses admiration, praise, sorrow, or joy, and in this context lends a mystical meaning to the poem, for the *nazuna* is the most common and insignificant of flowers.

7

Love and Beauty Mystics

It is generally observed that the Mystic writers had staunch penchant for love and beauty, which they took as supernatural/metaphysical way.

Here in this chapter we will address to love and beauty mystics of literature.

The thought of mysticism has endless ability to capture the imagination. The immediate mental picture is of bliss, exalted thought, and insights denied those not privileged to have the gift. There is a certain truth to these concepts, but, as we shall see, the definition of this reality may be far from what appears at first glance.

It is pertinent to note that the medieval mind was perhaps unequalled for imagery, romance, and poetic expression. Until Petrarch began dedicating his poetry to an earthly love, artistic and literary works focussed on religious images. Those in the Middle Ages were frequently illiterate, and undoubtedly uninfluenced by the writings of the great theologians of the period, yet their entertainment, legends, ballads, and so forth painted a vivid picture of God's active presence in the lives of His creatures. The true mystic will never be understood, and those honoured as saints were likely, then and now, to be remembered more for what they accomplished (or for what their intercession is thought to obtain for their devotees!) than for their mysterious and often troubling focus on the divine.

Many a mystic, Francis of Assisi being a prime example, is gifted in expression, yet the fullness of their union with God leaves us puzzled. Total unity goes beyond the senses and the intellect, and the greatest of poets is rendered silent by the inability to fully share the inexpressible.

In fact, Christian mysticism sees growth in spirituality as involving an ever deepening, personal relationship with God. The mystic, whose longing for a total bond with the Beloved, is not seeking nothingness, nor to "find the God within." His Lover is also a Person, albeit one Divine. Since true contemplation is a gift of grace from God Himself, the mystic remains fully (and, perhaps, anxiously) aware that his own accomplishments and efforts cannot attain this union.

Since the emphasis at this site is on delight, it is time to expand the definition! The mystic indeed delights in his Beloved, but this takes him into new realms. The human need for satisfaction of the mind and emotions is ever part of our nature, yet the mystic is dealing with pure spirit, unfathomable intellect, perfection beyond human grasp. He will see the emptiness of the world and the limits of our own perceptions. Thus, the lover's longing, which in itself is a sheer gift of grace, meets with silence. Unchanging, eternal, perfect love surely is the ultimate delight, but the mystic, hampered by the clouded vision of mankind, has both total dedication and the unrequited longing that cannot be satisfied in this world. Growth in Christian spirituality involves several stages, described as the purgative, illuminative, and unitive ways. An in-depth treatment of these stages is beyond the scope of this essay, but a brief reference is needed to place the mystic journey in perspective. Where the thought of meditation or prayer brings to mind actions of the mind, body (as in observing quiet), senses, and intellect, the way of the mystic is based on submission of the will. His journey begins with a renunciation of sin, that will, in time, lead to a certain darkness.

The mystic sees the Scriptures, the teachings of Christ's Church and the writings of Her mystics, and so forth as divine revelation - and, since they spring from a perfect source, will intuitively realise that there can be no surer path to happiness. His own heightened vision of divine love (of which he usually is unaware) will leave him troubled, because the reality of evil and indifference taps the human sense of futility and emptiness in this world.

The mystic, of course, is totally unaware of his "stage of development". The growing detachment, so essential to the eventual mystic union, will leave his senses and mind with further emptiness. The will, which alone can choose and love, is assuredly turned to God, yet there is much more to human nature - and that part remains unsatisfied, until the level of detachment is one attained by few. This is a process for a lifetime. The mystic, who will begin with the self knowledge from which humility is born, but eventually reaches the uncharted paths of that heightened vision that only the divine can inspire, will have continuously advancing awareness of his own nothingness. This "nothingness" is real - and by no means negative, even if it appears so to our post Freudian eyes.

If humans are created in the image and likeness of God (that is, with a memory, intellect, and will, and an immortal soul), and Christ Himself could assume human nature, clearly humanity is a great treasure in itself. However, when one has had a glimpse of the Perfect, the limits of human nature are clear to him. This void naturally is to be filled with that share in God that we call divine grace. Still, when one burns with a love that cannot be fully consummated except in a life beyond this one, the lover naturally will endure trials and the fire of longing that only those who truly love can know.

Looking for the God within, should a mystic fall into this error, would satisfy none of the longing. The divine essence within each creature is very limited. To turn the fire of mystic longing totally within would accomplish nothing - except, perhaps, to lead him to the error of worshipping himself. The constant striving for virtue, whether through prayer or the sacrifices typical of the ascetic life that alone is the bridge to the mystical, aims at pleasing the Creator, with whom the personal relationship constantly grows. Medieval man would hardly have grasped this concept, but he did understand, in his homely fashion, that God's love cannot be placed in a far off box. The Catholic concept of the "communion of saints" was known, even if all but the scholars would have been hard put to define this. The man of the Middle Ages had a strong idea of there being a life beyond this one - indeed, that awareness was sustenance in a time when life was short and filled with trials.

He also would have the idea that all of those who shared in grace (in this life or the next, the only exception being the devils and human inhabitants of hell) merit graces and grieve for sin as a whole. He would not have understood the depth of mysticism, of course, but he would value the mystic for the graces that these chosen ones merited for the sake of all, much as Christ had attained redemption for the sins of all people (with no bounds of time). The medieval imagination, coupled with the awareness of powers beyond one's self, was hardly confined to divine truths! The occult arts, the wee folk, the goblin and the "beasties" were forces to be reckoned with - and much a part of the medieval viewpoint. Then as now, the key difference between magic and spirituality is easy to overlook. The magic arts, to use one inclusive term, all are directed, in some fashion, at enhanced power for the individual. The intentions are not necessarily evil, but always include knowing, doing, or causing what is beyond normal human ability.

Spirituality, by contrast, and in a way that can be frightening to us since the desire for control is so a part of our nature, involves abandonment. With submission of the will being the key element of mystic union (and one against which we all shall struggle!), abandonment is transformed, in the mystic's vision, from a frightful struggle to a loving union. The mystic's heightened awareness, so incomprehensible to the rest of us, leads to a knowledge that nothing will satisfy him except God. He will have the pain of being unable to take pleasure in the worldly, but his will shall consider these well sacrificed in light of the ecstasy of eternity.

It worth to quote Saint Augustine who wrote in his "Confessions":

> "O Lord, do I love Thee. Thou didst strike on my heart with Thy word and I loved Thee.... But what do I love when I love Thee? Not the beauty of bodies nor the loveliness of seasons, nor the radiance of the light around us, so gladsome to our eyes, nor the sweet melodies of songs of every kind, nor the fragrance of flowers and ointments and spices, nor manna and honey, nor limbs delectable for fleshly embraces. I do not love these things when I love my God. And yet I love a light and a voice and a fragrance and a food and an embrace when I love my God, who is a light, a voice, a fragrance, a food, and an embrace to my inner man.... This it is that I love when I love my God...
>
> That same voice speaks indeed to all men, but only they understand it who join that voice, heard from outside, to the truth that is within them. And the truth says to me: "Neither heaven nor earth nor any body is thy God." Their own nature says the same They see that the substance of a part is less than that of the whole. And now I speak to thee, my soul. Thou art my greater part, since thou quickenest the substance of my body by giving to it life, which no body can give to a body. And thy God is the life of thy life to thee....

> Late have I loved Thee, O Beauty so ancient and so new! Too late have I loved Thee. And lo, Thou wert inside me and I outside, and I sought for Thee there, and in all my unsightliness I flung myself on those beautiful things which Thou hast made. Thou wert with me and I was not with Thee. Those beauties kept me away from Thee, though if they had not been in Thee, they would not have been at all. Thou didst call and cry to me and break down my deafness. Thou didst flash and shine on me and put my blindness to flight. Thou didst blow fragrance upon me and I drew breath, and now I pant after Thee. I tasted of Thee and now I hunger and thirst for Thee. Thou didst touch me and I am aflame for Thy peace...."

In studying the mysticism of the English writers, and more especially of the poets, one is at once struck by the diversity of approach leading to unity of end. "There are," says Plotinus, "different roads by which this end [apprehension of the Infinite] may be reached. The love of beauty, which exalts the poet; that devotion to the One and that ascent of science which makes the ambition of the philosopher; and that love and those prayers by which some devout and ardent soul tends in its moral purity towards perfection. These are the great highways conducting to that height above the actual and the particular, where we stand in the immediate presence of the Infinite, who shines out as from the deeps of the soul."—*Letter to Flaccus.*

Remarkably, we have grouped together English writers who are mystical in thought, according to the five main pathways by which they have seen the Vision: Love, Beauty, Nature, Wisdom, or Devotion. Even within these groups, the method of approach, the interpretation or application of the Idea, often differs very greatly. For instance, Shelley and Browning may both be called love-mystics; that is, they look upon love as the solution of the mystery of life, as the link between God and man.

To Shelley this was a glorious intuition, which reached him through his imagination, whereas the life of man as he saw it roused in him little but mad indignation, wild revolt, and passionate protest. To Browning this was knowledge—knowledge borne in upon him just because of human life as he saw it, which to him was a clear proof of the great destiny of the race. He would have agreed with Patmore that "you can see the disc of Divinity quite clearly through the smoked glass of humanity, but no otherwise." He found "harmony in immortal souls, spite of the muddy vesture of decay."

In fact, the three great English poets who are also fundamentally mystical in thought are Browning, Wordsworth, and Blake. Their philosophy or mystical belief, one in essence, though so differently expressed, lies at the root, as it is also the flower, of their life-work. In others, as in Shelley, Keats, and Rossetti, although it is the inspiring force of their poetry, it is not a flame, burning steadily and evenly, but rather a light flashing out intermittently into brilliant and dazzling radiance. Hence the man himself is not so permeated by it; and hence results the unsatisfied desire, the almost painful yearning, the recurring disappointment and disillusionment, which we do not find in Browning, Wordsworth, and Blake.

In the first group we have four poets of markedly different temperaments—Shelley intensely spiritual; Rossetti with a strong tinge of sensuousness, of "earthiness" in his nature; Browning, the keenly intellectual man of the world, and Patmore a curious mixture of materialist and mystic; yet to all four love is the secret of life, the one thing worth giving and possessing. Shelley believed in a Soul of the Universe, a Spirit in which all things live and move and have their being; which, as one feels in the *Prometheus*, is unnamable, inconceivable even to man, for "the deep truth is imageless." His most passionate desire was not, as was Browning's, for an increased and ennobled individuality, but for the mystical fusion of his own personality with this

Spirit, this object of his worship and adoration. To Shelley, death itself was but the rending of a veil which would admit us to the full vision of the ideal, which alone is true life. The sense of unity in all things is most strongly felt in *Adonais*, where Shelley's maturest thought and philosophy are to be found; and indeed the mystical fervour in this poem, especially towards the end, is greater than anywhere else in his writings.

The *Hymn to Intellectual Beauty* is in some ways Shelley's clearest and most obvious expression of his devotion to the Spirit of Ideal Beauty, its reality to him, and his vow of dedication to its service. But the *Prometheus* is the most deeply mystical of his poems; indeed, as Mrs Shelley says, "it requires a mind as subtle and penetrating as Shelley's own to understand the mystic meanings scattered throughout the poem."

Shelley, like Blake, regarded the human imagination as a divine creative force; Prometheus stands for the human imagination, or the genius of the world; and it is his union with Asia, the divine Idea, the Spirit of Beauty and of Love, from which a new universe is born. It is this union, which consummates the aspirations of humanity, that Shelley celebrates in the marvellous love-song of Prometheus. As befitted a disciple of Godwin, he believed in the divine potentiality of man, convinced that all good is to be found within man's own being, and that his progress depends on his own will.

> It is our will
> That thus enchains us to permitted ill—
> We might be otherwise—we might be all
> We dream of happy, high, majestical.
> Where is the love, beauty, and truth we seek
> But in our mind?
> *Julian and Maddalo.*

It is significant to note that in the allegorical introduction to the *Revolt of Islam*, which is an interesting example of Shelley's mystical mythology, we have an insight into the poet's view of the good power in the world. It is not an almighty creator standing outside mankind, but a power which suffers and rebels and evolves, and is, in fact, incarnate in humanity, so that it is unrecognised by men, and indeed confounded with evil:—

> And the Great Spirit of Good did creep among
> The nations of mankind, and every tongue
> Cursed and blasphemed him as he passed, for none
> Knew good from evil.

No doubt, to Shelley the form assumed by the divine in man was love. Mrs Shelley, in her note to *Rosalind and Helen*, says that, "in his eyes it was the essence of our being, and all woe and pain arose from the war made against it by selfishness or insensibility, or mistake"; and Shelley himself says, "the great secret of morals is love; or a going out of our own nature, and an identification of ourselves with the beautiful which exists in thought, action or person, not our own."

In fact, Shelley was always searching for love; and, although he knew well, through his study of Plato, the difference between earthly and spiritual love, that the one is but the lowest step on the ladder which leads to the other, yet in actual practice he confounded the two. He knew that he did so; and only a month before his death, he summed up in a sentence the tragedy of his life. He writes to Mr Gisborne about the *Epipsychidion*, saying that he cannot look at it now, for—

> "the person whom it celebrates was a cloud instead of a Juno," and continues, "If you are curious, however, to hear what I am and have been, it will tell you something thereof. It is an idealized history of my life and feelings. I think one is always in love with something or other; the error—and I

confess it is not easy for spirits cased in flesh and blood to avoid it—consists in seeking in a mortal image the likeness of what is, perhaps, eternal."

Remarkably, no poet has a more distinct philosophy of life than Browning. Indeed he has as much a right to a place among the philosophers, as Plato has to one among the poets. Browning is a seer, and pre-eminently a mystic; and it is especially interesting as in the case of Plato and St Paul, to encounter this latter quality as a dominating characteristic of the mind of so keen and logical a dialectician. We see at once that the main position of Browning's belief is identical with what we have found to be the characteristic of mysticism—unity under diversity at the centre of all existence.

The same essence, the one life, expresses itself through every diversity of form.

He dwells on this again and again:—

God is seen
In the star, in the stone, in the flesh, in the soul and the clod.

And through all these forms there is growth upwards. Indeed, it is only upon this supposition that the poet can account for

many a thrill
Of kinship, I confess to, with the powers
Called Nature: animate, inanimate
In parts or in the whole, there's something there
Man-like that somehow meets the man in me.

—*Prince Hohenstiel-Schwangau.*

In fact, the poet sees that in each higher stage we benefit by the garnered experience of the past; and so man grows and expands and becomes capable of feeling for and with everything that lives. At the same time the higher is not degraded by having worked in and through the lower, for he distinguishes between the continuous persistent life, and the temporary coverings it makes use of on its upward way;

> From first to last of lodging, I was I,
> And not at all the place that harboured me.

Humanity then, in Browning's view, is not a collection of individuals, separate and often antagonistic, but one whole.

> When I say "you" 'tis the common soul,
> The collective I mean: the race of Man
> That receives life in parts to live in a whole
> And grow here according to God's clear plan.
> *Old Pictures in Florence.*

This sense of unity is shown in many ways: for instance, in Browning's protest against the one-sidedness of nineteenth-century scientific thought, the sharp distinction or gulf set up between science and religion. This sharp cleavage, to the mystic, is impossible. He knows, however irreconcilable the two may appear, that they are but different aspects of the same thing. This is one of the ways in which Browning anticipates the most advanced thought of the present day.

In *Paracelsus* he emphasises the fact that the exertion of power in the intelligence, or the acquisition of knowledge, is useless without the inspiration of love, just as love is waste without power. Paracelsus sums up the matter when he says to Aprile—

> I too have sought to KNOW as thou to LOVE
> Excluding love as thou refusedst knowledge....
> We must never part ...
> Till thou the lover, know; and I, the knower,
> Love—until both are saved.

Arising logically out of this belief in unity, there follows, as with all mystics, the belief in the potential divinity of man, which permeates all Browning's thought, and is continually insisted on in such poems as *Rabbi ben Ezra, A Death in the Desert*, and *The Ring and the Book*. He takes for granted the fundamental position of the mystic, that the object of life is to know God; and according to the poet, in knowing love we learn to know God. Hence it follows that love is the meaning of life, and that he who finds it not

> loses what he lived for
> And eternally must lose it.
> *Christina.*
> For life with all it yields of joy and woe
> And hope and fear ...
> Is just our chance o' the prize of learning love.
> *A Death in the Desert.*

This is Browning's central teaching, the key-note of his work and philosophy. The importance of love in life is to Browning supreme, because he holds it to be the meeting-point between God and man. Love is the sublimest conception possible to man; and a life inspired by it is the highest conceivable form of goodness. In this exaltation of love, as in several other points, Browning much resembles the German mystic, Meister Eckhart. To compare the two writers in detail would be an interesting task; it is only possible here to suggest points of resemblance. The following passage from Eckhart suggests several directions in which Browning's thought is peculiarly mystical:—

> "Intelligence is the youngest faculty in man.... The soul in itself is a simple work; what God works in the simple light of the soul is more beautiful and more delightful than all the other works which He works in all creatures. But foolish people take evil for good and good for evil. But to him who

> rightly understands, the one work which God works in the soul is better and nobler and higher than all the world. Through that light comes grace. Grace never comes in the intelligence or in the will. If it could come in the intelligence or in the will, the intelligence and the will would have to transcend themselves. On this a master says: There is something secret about it; and thereby he means the spark of the soul, which alone can apprehend God. The true union between God and the soul takes place in the little spark, which is called the spirit of the soul."

Remarkably, essential unity of God and man is expressed more than once by Browning in Eckhart's image: as when he speaks of God as Him

> Who never is dishonoured in the spark
> He gave us from his fire of fires.

As such, is at one with Eckhart, and with all mystics, in his appeal from the intellect to that which is beyond intellect; in his assertion of the supremacy of feeling, intuition, over knowledge. Browning never wearies of dwelling on the relativity of physical knowledge, and its inadequacy to satisfy man. This is perhaps best brought out in one of the last things he wrote, the "Reverie" in *Asolando*; but it is dwelt on in nearly all his later and more reflective poems. His maxim was—

> Wholly distrust thy knowledge, then, and trust
> As wholly love allied to ignorance!
> There lies thy truth and safety. ...
> Consider well!
> Were knowledge all thy faculty, then God
> Must be ignored: love gains him by first leap.
> *A Pillar at Sebzevar.*

It is pertinent to note that another point of resemblance

with Eckhart is suggested by his words: "That foolish people take evil for good, and good for evil." Browning's theory of evil is part of the working-out of his principle of what may be called the coincidence of extreme opposites. This is, of course, part of his main belief in unity, but it is an interesting development of it.

This theory is marked all through his writings; and, although philosophers have dealt with it, he is perhaps the one poet who faces the problem, and expresses himself on the point with entire conviction.

His view is that good and evil are purely relative terms, and that one cannot exist without the other. It is evil which alone makes possible some of the divinest qualities in man—compassion, pity, forgiveness patience. We have seen that Shelley shares this view, "for none knew good from evil"; and Blake expresses himself very strongly about it, and complains that Plato "knew nothing but the virtues and vices, the good and evil.... There is nothing in all that.... Everything is good in God's eyes."

Mysticism is always a reconcilement of opposites; and this, as we have seen in connection with science and religion, knowledge and love, is a dominant note of Browning's philosophy. He brings it out most startlingly perhaps in *The Statue and the Bust*, where he shows that in his very capacity for vice, a man proves his capacity for virtue, and that a failure of energy in the one implies a corresponding failure of energy in the other.

At the same time, clear knowledge that evil is illusion would defeat its own end and paralyse all moral effort, for evil only exists for the development of good in us.

This is one reason why Browning never shrank from the evil in the world, why indeed he expended so much of his mind and art on the analysis and dissection of every kind of evil, laying bare for us the working of the mind of the criminal, the hypocrite, the weakling, and the cynic; because he held that—

Only by looking low, ere looking high
Comes penetration of the mystery.

There are other ways in which Browning's thought is especially mystical, as, for instance, his belief in pre-existence, and his theory of knowledge, for he, like Plato, believes in the light within the soul, and holds that—

To know
Rather consists in opening out a way
Whence the imprisoned splendour may escape,
Than in effecting entry for a light
Supposed to be without.
Paracelsus, Act I.

But the one thought which is ever constant with him, and is peculiarly helpful to the practical man, is his recognition of the value of limitation in all our energies, and the stress he lays on the fact that only by virtue of this limitation can we grow. We should be paralysed else. It is Goethe's doctrine of *Entbehrung*, and it is vividly portrayed in the epistle of Karshish. Paracelsus learns it, and makes it clear to Festus at the end.

The natural result of Browning's theory of evil, and his sense of the value of limitation, is that he should welcome for man the experience of doubt, difficulty, temptation, pain; and this we find is the case.

Life is probation and the earth no goal
But starting point of man...
To try man's foot, if it will creep or climb
'Mid obstacles in seeming, points that prove
Advantage for who vaults from low to high
And makes the stumbling-block a stepping-stone.
The Ring and the Book: The Pope, 1436-7, 410-13.

It is this trust in unending progress, based on the

consciousness of present failure, which is peculiarly inspiriting in Browning's thought, and it is essentially mystical. Instead of shrinking from pain, the mystic prays for it, for, properly met, it means growth.

> Was the trial sore?
> Temptation sharp? Thank God a second time!
> Why comes temptation but for man to meet
> And master and make crouch beneath his foot,
> And so be pedestaled in triumph?
> *The Ring and the Book*: The Pope, 1182-02.

Similarly, Rossetti's mysticism is perhaps a more salient feature in his art than is the case with Browning, and the lines of it, and its place in his work, have been well described by Mr Theodore Watts-Dutton. We can only here indicate wherein it lies, and how it differs from and falls short of the mysticism of Shelley and Browning. Rossetti, unlike Browning, is not the least metaphysical; he is not devoured by philosophical curiosity; he has no desire to solve the riddle of the universe. All his life he was dominated and fascinated by beauty, one form of which in especial so appealed to him as at times almost to overpower him—the beauty of the face of woman. But this beauty is not an end in itself; it is not the desire of possession that so stirs him, but rather an absolute thirst for the knowledge of the mystery which he feels is hiding beneath and beyond it. Here lies his mysticism.

It is this haunting passion which is the greatest thing in Rossetti, which inspires all that is best in him as artist, the belief that beauty is but the expression or symbol of something far greater and higher, and that it has kinship with immortal things. For beauty, which, as Plato has told us, is of all the divine ideas at once most manifest and most lovable to man, is for Rossetti the actual and visible symbol of love, which is at once the mystery and solution of the secret of life. Rossetti's mystical passion is perhaps most perfectly expressed in his little early prose romance, *Hand and Soul*. It is purer and more austere than much of his poetry, and breathes an amazing force of spiritual vision. One wonders, after reading it, that the writer himself did not attain to a loftier and more spiritual development of life and art; and one cannot help feeling the reason was that he did not sufficiently heed the warning of Plotinus, not to let ourselves become entangled in sensuous beauty, which will engulf us as in a swamp. Coventry Patmore was so entirely a mystic that it seems to be the first and the last and the only thing to say about him. His central conviction is the unity of all things, and hence their mutual interpretation and symbolic force. There is only one kind of knowledge which counts with him, and that is direct apprehension or perception, the knowledge a man has of Love, by being in love, not by reading about its symptoms. The "touch" of God is not a figure of speech.

"Touch," says Aquinas, "applies to spiritual things as well as to material things.... The fulness of intelligence is the obliteration of intelligence. God is then our honey, and we, as St Augustine says, are His; and who wants to understand honey or requires the *rationale* of a kiss?" (*Rod, Root, and Flower*, xx.)

Once given the essential idea, to be grasped by the intuitive faculty alone, the world is full of analogies, of natural revelations which help to support and illustrate great truths. Patmore was, however, caught and enthralled by one aspect of unity, by one great analogy, almost to the exclusion of all others. This is that in human love, but above all in wedded love, we have a symbol (that is an expression of a similar force in different material) of the love between God and the soul.

What Patmore meant was that in the relationship and attitude of wedded lovers we hold the key to the mystery at the heart of life, and that we have in it a "real apprehension" (which is quite different from real comprehension) of the relationship and attitude of humanity to God. His first wife's love revealed to him this, which is the basic fact of all his thought and work.

The relationship of the soul to Christ *as His betrothed wife* is the key to the feeling with which prayer and love and honour should be offered to Him ... *She* showed me what that relationship involves of heavenly submission and spotless passionate loyalty. He believed that sex is a relationship at the base of all things natural and divine.

Nature, with endless being rife,
 Parts each thing into "him" and "her"
And, in the arithmetic of life,
 The smallest unit is a pair.

Basically, this division into two and reconciliation into one, this clash of forces resulting in life, is, as Patmore points out in words curiously reminiscent of those of Boehme, at the root of all existence. All real apprehension of God, he says, is dependent upon the realisation of his triple Personality in one Being.

Nature goes on giving echoes of the same living triplicity in animal, plant, and mineral, every stone and material atom owing its being to the synthesis or "embrace" of the two opposed forces of expansion and contraction. Nothing whatever exists in a single entity but in virtue of its being thesis, antithesis, and synthesis and in humanity and natural life this takes the form of sex, the masculine, the feminine, and the neuter, or third, forgotten sex spoken of by Plato, which is not the absence of the life of sex, but its fulfilment and power, as the electric fire is the fulfilment and power of positive and negative in their "embrace."

God he conceived of as the great masculine positive force, the soul as the feminine or receptive force, and the meeting of these two, the "mystic rapture" of the marriage of Divinity and Humanity, as the source of all life and joy.

This profound and very difficult theme is treated by Patmore in a manner at once austere and passionate in the exquisite little preludes to the *Angel in the House*, and more especially in the odes, which stand alone in nineteenth-century poetry for poignancy of feeling and depth of spiritual passion. They are the highest expression of "erotic mysticism" in English; a marvellous combination of flaming ardour and sensuousness of description with purity and austerity of tone. This latter effect is gained largely by the bare and irregular metre, which has a curiously compelling beauty of rhythm and dignity of cadence.

The book into which Patmore put the fullness of his convictions, the *Sponsa Dei*, which he burnt because he feared it revealed too much to a world not ready for it, was says Mr Gosse, who had read it in manuscript, "a transcendental treatise on Divine desire seen through the veil of human desire." We can guess fairly accurately its tenor and spirit if we read the prose essay *Dieu et ma Dame* and the wonderful ode *Sponsa Dei*, which, happily, the poet did not destroy.

It may be noted that the other human affections and relationships also have for Patmore a deep symbolic value, and two of his finest odes are written, the one in symbolism of mother love, the other in that of father and son. We learn by human love, so be points out, to realise the possibility of contact between the finite and Infinite, for divinity can only be revealed by voluntarily submitting to limitations. It is "the mystic craving of the great to become the love-captive of the small, while the small has a corresponding thirst for the enthralment of the great." And this process of intercourse between God and man is symbolised in the Incarnation, which is not a single event in time, but the culmination of an eternal process. It is the central fact of a man's experience, "for it is going on perceptibly in himself"; and in like manner "the Trinity becomes the only and self-evident explanation of mysteries which are daily wrought in his own complex nature." In this way is it that to

Patmore religion is not a question of blameless life or the holding of certain beliefs, but it is "an experimental science" to be lived and to be felt, and the clues to the experiments are to be found in natural human processes and experiences interpreted in the light of the great dogmas of the Christian faith.

For Keats, the avenue to truth and reality took the form of Beauty. The idea, underlying most deeply and consistently the whole of his poetry, is that of the unity of life; and closely allied with this is the belief in progress, through ever-changing, ever-ascending stages. *Sleep and Poetry, Endymion*, and *Hyperion* represent very well three stages in the poet's thought and art.

In *Sleep and Poetry* Keats depicts the growth even in an individual life, and describes the three stages of thought, or attitudes towards life, through which the poet must pass. They are not quite parallel to the three stages of the mystical ladder marked out by Wordsworth in the main body of his poetry, because they do not go quite so far, but they are almost exactly analogous to the three stages of mind he describes in *Tintern Abbey*.

The first is mere animal pleasure and delight in living—

A pigeon tumbling in clear summer air;
A laughing school-boy without grief or care
Hiding the springy branches of an elm.

Then follows simple unreflective enjoyment of Nature. The next stage is sympathy with human life, with human grief and joy, which brings a sense of the mystery of the world, a longing to pierce it and arrive at its meaning, symbolised in the figure of the charioteer. Towards the end of Keats's life this feeling was growing stronger; and it is much dwelt upon in the *Revision of Hyperion*. There he plainly states that the merely artistic life, the life of the dreamer, is selfish; and that the only way to gain real insight is through contact and sympathy with human suffering and sorrow; and in the lost Woodhouse transcript of the *Revision*, rediscovered in 1904, there are some lines in which this point is still further emphasised. The full realisation of this third stage was not granted to Keats during his short life; he had but gleams of it.

The only passage where he describes the ecstasy of vision is in *Endymion* (bk. i., 1. 774 ff.), and this resembles in essentials all the other reports of this experience given by mystics. When the mind is ready, anything may lead us to it—music, imagination, love, friendship.

> Feel we these things?—that moment have we stept
> Into a sort of oneness, and our state
> Is like a floating spirit's.

Keats felt this passage was inspired, and in a letter to Taylor in January 1818 he says, "When I wrote it, it was a regular stepping of the Imagination towards a truth." In *Endymion*, the underlying idea is the unity of the various elements of the individual soul; the love of woman is shown to be the same as the love of beauty; and that in its turn is identical with the love of the principle of beauty in all things. Keats was always very sensitive to the mysterious effects of moonlight, and so for him the moon became a symbol for the great abstract principle of beauty, which, during the whole of his poetic life, he worshipped intellectually and spiritually. "The mighty abstract Idea I have of Beauty in all things stifles the more divided and minute domestic happiness," he writes to his brother George; and the last two well-known lines of the *Ode on a Grecian Urn* fairly sum up his philosophy—

> Beauty is truth, truth Beauty, that is all
> Ye know on earth, and all ye need to know.

So that the moon represents to Keats the eternal idea, the one essence in all. This is how he writes of it, in what is an entirely mystical passage in *Endymion*—

... As I grew in years, still didst thou blend
With all my ardours: thou wast the deep glen;
Thou wast the mountain-top, the sage's pen,
The poet's harp, the voice of friends, the sun;
Thou wast the river, thou wast glory won;
Thou wast my clarion's blast, thou wast my steed,
My goblet full of wine, my topmost deed:
Thou wast the charm of women, lovely Moon!

Similarly, in his fragment of *Hyperion*, Keats shadows forth the unity of all existence, and gives magnificent utterance to the belief that change is not decay, but the law of growth and progress.

8

Philosophical Mysticism

Basically 'mysticism' is a term of philosophy, frequently used to delineate spirituality, panthcism and supernaturalism.

It is pertinent to note that the mystical sense may be called philosophical in all those writers who present their convictions in a philosophic form calculated to appeal to the intellect as well as to the emotions. These writers, as a rule, though not always, are themselves markedly intellectual, and their primary concern therefore is with truth or wisdom. Thus Donne, William Law, Burke, Coleridge, and Carlyle are all predominantly intellectual, while Traherne, Emily Brontë, and Tennyson clothe their thoughts to some extent in the language of philosophy. The dominating characteristic of Donne is intellectuality; and this may partly account for the lack in him of some essentialty mystical qualities, more especially reverence, and that ascension of thought so characteristic of Plato and Browning. These shortcomings are very well illustrated in that extraordinary poem, *The, Progress of the Soul*. The idea is a mystical one, derived from Pythagorean philosophy, and has great possibilities, which Donne entirely fails to utilise; for, instead of following the soul upwards on its way, he depicts it as merely jumping about from body to body, and we are conscious of an entire lack of any lift or grandeur of thought.

This poem helps us to understand how it was that Donne, though so richly endowed with intellectual gifts, yet failed to reach the highest rank as a poet. He was brilliant in particulars, but lacked the epic qualities of breadth, unity, and proportion, characteristics destined to be the distinctive marks of the school of which he is looked upon as the founder.

Apart from this somewhat important defect, Donne's attitude of mind is essentially mystical. This is especially marked in his feeling about the body and natural law, in his treatment of love, and in his conception of woman. The mystic's postulate—if we could know ourselves, we should know all—is often on Donne's lips, as for instance in that curious poem written in memory of Elizabeth Drury, on the second anniversary of her death. It is perhaps best expressed in the following verse:

> But we know our selves least; Mere outward shews
> Our mindes so store,
> That our soules, no more than our eyes disclose
> But forme and colour. Onely he who knowes
> Himselfe, knowes more.
> *Ode: Of our Sense of Sinne.*

One of the marked characteristics of Donne's poetry is his continual comparison of mental and spiritual with, physical processes. This sense of analogy prevailing throughout nature is with him very strong. The mystery of continual flux and change particularly attracts him, as it did the Buddhists and the early Greek thinkers, and Nettleship's remarks about the nature of bread and unselfishness are akin to the following comparison:—

> Dost thou love
> Beauty? (And beauty worthy'st is to move)
> Poor cousened consener, *that* she, and *that* thou,
> Which did begin to love, are neither now;
> Next day repaires (but ill) last dayes decay.
> Nor are, (although the river keepe the name)

Yesterdaies waters, and to-daies the same.
Of the Progresse of the Soule. The second Anniversarie, 389-96.

Donne believes firmly in man's potential greatness, and the power within his own soul:

Seeke wee then our selves in our selves; for as
Men force the Sunne with much more force to passe.
By gathering his beames with a chrystall glasse;
So wee, If wee into our selves will turne,
Blowing our sparkes of virtue, may out-burne
The straw, which doth about our hearts sojourne.
Letter to Mr Roland Woodward.

And although, in the *Progress of the Soul*, he failed to give expression to it, yet his belief in progress is unquenchable. He fully shares the mystic's view that "man, to get towards Him that's Infinite, must first be great" (*Letter to the Countess of Salisbury*).

In his treatment of love, Donne's mystical attitude is most clearly seen. He holds the Platonic conception, that love concerns the soul only, and is independent of the body, or bodily presence; and he is the poet, who, at his best, expresses this idea in the most dignified and refined way. The reader feels not only that Donne believes it, but that he has in some measure experienced it; whereas with his imitators it degenerated into little more than a fashionable "conceit." The *Undertaking* expresses the discovery he has made of this higher and deeper kind of love; and in the *Ecstasy* he describes the union of the souls of two lovers in language which proves his familiarity with the description of ecstasy given by Plotinus (*Enn.* vi. 9, § 11). The great value of this spiritual love is that it is unaffected by time and space, a belief which is nowhere more exquisitely expressed than in the refrain of his little song, *Soul's Joy*.

O give no way to griefe,
But let beliefe
Of mutuall love,
This wonder to the vulgar prove
Our Bodyes, not wee move.

In one of his verse letters to the Countess of Huntingdon he explains how true love cannot be desire:

'Tis love, but with such fatall weaknesse made,
That it destroyes it selfe with its owne shade.

He goes still further in the poem entitled *Negative Love*, where he says that love is such a passion as can only be defined by negatives, for it is above apprehension, and his language here is closely akin to the description of the One or the Good given by Plotinus in the sixth Ennead.

Thomas Traherne is a mystical writer of singular charm and originality. The manuscripts of his poems and his prose *Meditations*, a kind of spiritual autobiography and notebook, were only discovered and printed quite recently, and they form a valuable addition to the mystical literature of the seventeenth century.

He has affinities with Vaughan, Herbert, and Sir Thomas Browne, with Blake and with Wordsworth. He is deeply sensitive to the beauty of the natural world, and he insists on the necessity for rejoicing in this beauty if we are really to live. By love alone is God to be approached and known, he says, but this love must not be finite. "He must be loved in all with an unlimited love, even in all His doings, in all His friends, in all His creatures." In a prose passage of sustained beauty Traherne thus describes the attitude towards earth which is needful before we can enter heaven.

You never enjoy the world aright, till the Sea itself floweth in your veins, till you are clothed with the heavens, and crowned with the stars:.... Till you can sing and rejoice and delight in God, as misers do in gold, and Kings in sceptres, you never enjoy the world.

Till your spirit filleth the whole world, and the stars are your jewels;.... till you love men so as to desire their happiness, with a thirst equal to the zeal of your own: till you delight in God for being good to all: you never enjoy the world.... The world is a mirror of infinite beauty, yet no man sees it. It is a Temple of Majesty, yet no man regards it. It is a region of Light and Peace, did not men disquiet it. It is the Paradise of God.... It is, the place of Angels and the Gate of Heaven.

He is for ever reiterating, in company with all the mystics, that

> 'Tis not the object, but the light
> That maketh Heaven: 'tis a purer sight.

He shares Wordsworth's rapture in the life of nature, and Browning's interest in his fellow-men; he has Shelley's belief in the inner meaning of love, and much of Keats's worship of beauty, and he expresses this in an original and lyrical prose of quite peculiar and haunting beauty. He has embodied his main ideas, with a good deal of repetition both in prose and verse, but it is invariably the prose version, probably written first, which is the most arresting and vigorous.

His *Meditations* well repay careful study; they are full of wisdom and of an imaginative philosophy, expressed in pithy and telling form, which continually reminds the reader of Blake's *Proverbs of Hell*.

> To have no principles or to live beside them, is equally miserable.
>
> Philosophers are not those that speak but do great things.

> All men see the same objects, but do not equally understand them.
>
> Souls to souls are like apples, one being rotten rots another.

This kind of saying abounds on every page. Some of his more sustained philosophic passages are also noteworthy; such, for instance, is his comparison of the powers of the soul to the rays of the sun, which carry light in them unexpressed until they meet an object (*Meditations*, second century, No. 78). But Traherne's most interesting contribution to the psychology of mysticism is his account of his childhood and the "vision splendid" that he brought with him.

> I was a little stranger, which at my entrance into the world was saluted and surrounded with innumerable joys.... The corn was orient and immortal wheat, which never should be reaped, nor was ever sown. I thought it had stood from everlasting to everlasting. The dust and stones of the street were as precious as gold: the gates were at first the end of the world. The green trees when I saw them first ... transported and ravished me, their sweetness and unusual beauty made my heart to leap, and almost mad with ecstasy, they were such strange and wonderful things. The Men! O what venerable and reverend creatures did the aged seem! Immortal Cherubims! And young men glittering and sparkling Angels, and maids strange seraphic pieces of life and beauty! Boys and girls tumbling in the street, and playing, were moving jewels. I knew not that they were born or should die; but all things abided eternally as they were in their proper places.... The city seemed to stand in Eden, or to be built in Heaven.

It is necessary to quote at some length, because it is the way in which Traherne expresses his experiences or reflections which is the moving and original thing about him. This last passage seems to anticipate something of the magic of Keats in the *Ode to a Nightingale* or the *Grecian Urn*, the sense of continuity, and of eternity expressed in time. Traherne's account of the gradual dimming of this early radiance, and his enforced change of values is equally unusual. Only with great difficulty did his elders persuade him "that the tinselled ware upon a hobby-horse was a fine thing" and that a purse of gold was of any value, but by degrees when he found that all men prized things he did not dream of, and never mentioned those he cared for, then his "thoughts were blotted out; and at last all the celestial great and stable treasures, to which I was born, as wholly forgotten, if as they had never been."

But he remembered enough of those early glories to realise that if he would regain happiness, he must "become, as it were, a little child again," get free of "the burden and cumber of devised wants," and recapture the value and the glory of the common things of life. He was so resolutely bent on this that when he had left college and come into the country and was free, he lived upon £10 a year, fed on bread and water, and, like George Fox, wore a leather suit. Thus released from all worldly cares, he says, through God's blessing, "I live a free and kingly life as if the world were turned again into Eden, or much more, as it is at this day."

In Emily Brontë we have an unusual type of mystic. Indeed she is one of the most strange and baffling figures in our literature. We know in truth very little about her, but that little is quite unlike what we know about any one else. It is now beginning to be realised that she was a greater and more original genius than her famous sister, and that strong as were Charlotte's passion and imagination, the passion and imagination of Emily were still stronger. She had, so far as we can tell, peculiarly little actual experience of life, her material interests were bounded by her family, the old servant Tabby, the dogs, and the moors. For the greater part of her thirty years of life she did the work of a servant in the little parsonage house on the edge of the graveyard. She can have read little of philosophy or metaphysics, and probably had never heard of the mystics;

she was brought up in a narrow, crude, and harshly material creed; yet her own inner experience, her touch with the secret of life, enabled her to write the remarkable series of poems the peculiar and haunting quality of which has as yet scarcely been recognised.

They are strong and free and certain, hampered by no dogma, weighted by no explanation, but containing—in the simplest language—the record of the experience and the vision of a soul. Emily Brontë lived remote, unapproachable, self-sufficing and entirely detached, yet consumed with a fierce, unquenchable love of life and of nature, of the life which withheld from her all the gifts most prized of men, love, friendship, experience, recognition, fame; and of the nature which she knew only on a circumscribed space of the wild Yorkshire moors. In her poems her mysticism is seen principally in two ways: in her unerring apprehension of values, of the illusory quality of material things, even of the nature she so loved, together with the certain vision of the one Reality behind all forms. This, and her description of ecstasy, of the all-sufficing joy of the inner life of one who has tasted this experience, mark her out as being among those who have seen, and who know.

In *The Prisoner*, the speaker, a woman, is "confined in triple walls," yet in spite of bolts and bars and dungeon gloom she holds within herself an inextinguishable joy and unmeasured freedom brought to her every night by a "messenger."

> He comes with western winds, with evening's wandering airs,
> With that clear dusk of heaven that brings the thickest stars.
> Winds take a pensive tone, and stars a tender fire,
> And visions rise, and change, that kill me with desire.
>
> But, first, a hush of peace—a soundless calm descends;

The struggle of distress, and fierce impatience ends;
Mute music soothes my breast—unuttered harmony,
That I could never dream, till Earth was lost to me.
Then dawns the Invisible; the Unseen its truth reveals;
My outward sense is gone, my inward essence feels:
Its wings are almost free—its home, its harbour found,
Measuring the gulf, it stoops and dares the final bound.
Oh! dreadful is the check—intense the agony—
When the ear begins to hear, and the eye begins to see;
When the pulse begins to throb, the brain to think again;
The soul to feel the flesh, and the flesh to feel the chain.

This is the description—always unmistakable—of the supreme mystic experience, the joy of the outward flight, the pain of the return, and it could only have been written by one who in some measure had knowledge of it. This, together with the exquisite little poem *The Visionary*, which describes a similar experience, and *The Philosopher*, stand apart as expressions of spiritual vision, and are among the most perfect mystic poems in English. Her realisation of the meaning of common things, her knowledge that they hold the secret of the universe, and her crystallisation of this in verse, place her with Blake and Wordsworth.

In fact, What have those lonely mountains worth revealing? More glory and more grief than I can tell: The earth that wakes one human heart to feeling Can centre both the worlds of Heaven and Hell.

And finally, the sense of continuous life—one central, all-sustaining Life—of the oneness of God and man, has never been more nobly expressed than in what is her best-known poem, the last lines she ever wrote:—

O God within my breast,
Almighty, ever-present Deity!

Life—that in me has rest,
As I—undying Life—have power in Thee!

With wide-embracing love
Thy spirit animates eternal years,
Pervades and broods above,
Changes, sustains, dissolves, creates, and rears.
Though earth and man were gone,
And suns and universes ceased to be,
And Thou wert left alone,
Every existence would exist in Thee.

Remarkably, Tennyson differs widely from the other poets whom we are considering in this connection. He was not born with the mystical temperament, but, on the contrary, he had a long and bitter struggle with his own doubts and questionings before he wrested from them peace.

There is nothing of mystic calm or strength in the lines—

Oh, yet we trust that somehow good
Will be the final goal of ill.

He has no mystic rapture in Nature like Wordsworth,

I found Him not in world or sun
Or eagle's wing, or insect's eye;

no mystic interpretation of life as had Browning, no yearning for union with the spirit of love and beauty as had Shelley. Tennyson's mysticism came, as it were, rather in spite of himself, and is based on one thing only—experience. He states his position quite clearly in *In Memoriam*, cxxiv. As is well known, he had from time to time a certain peculiar experience, which he describes fully both in prose and verse, a touch at intervals throughout his life of "ecstasy," and it was on this he based his deepest belief. He has left several prose accounts of this mental state, which often came to him through repeating his own name silently, till all at once, as it wore, out of the intensity of the consciousness of individuality, the individuality itself seemed to resolve and fade away into boundless being, and this not a confused state, but the clearest of the clearest, the surest of the surest, utterly beyond words, where death was an almost laughable impossibility, the loss of personality seeming no extinction, but the only true life

In fact, it is a somewhat similar experience which is described in *In Memoriam*, xcv.

And all at once it seem'd at last
The living soul was flash'd on mine,
And mine in this was wound, and whirl'd
About empyreal heights of thought,
And came on that which is, and caught
The deep pulsations of the world.

And again in the conclusion of the *Holy Grail*—

Let visions of the night or of the day
Come, as they will; and many a time they come,
Until this earth he walks on seems not earth,
This light that strikes his eyeball is not light,
This air that strikes his forehead is not air
But vision—yea, his very hand and foot—
In moments when he feels he cannot die,
And knows himself no vision to himself,
Nor the high God a A vision, nor that One
Who rose again.

"These three lines," said Tennyson, speaking of the last three quoted, "are the (spiritually) central lines in the Idylls." They are also the central lines in his own philosophy, for it was the experience of this "vision" that inspired all his deepest convictions with regard to the unity of all things, the reality of the unseen, and the persistence of life. The belief in the impotence of intellectual knowledge is very closely connected, it is indeed based, upon these "gleams" of ecstasy. The prologue to *In Memoriam* (written when the poem was completed) seems to sum up his faith after many years of struggle and doubt; but it is in the most philosophical as well as one of the latest, of his poems.

The Ancient Sage, that we find this attitude most fully expressed. Tennyson wrote of it: "The whole poem is very personal. The passages about 'Faith' and 'the Passion of the Past' were more especially my own personal feelings." Through the mouth of the Sage, the poet declares in impassioned words the position of the mystic, and points out the impotence of sense-knowledge in dealing with that which is beyond either the senses or the reason:

For Knowledge is the swallow on the lake
That sees and stirs the surface-shadow there
But never yet hath dipt into the abysm.

In fact, Tennyson, like Wordsworth, emphasises the truth that the only way in which man can gain real knowledge and hear the "Nameless" is by diving or sinking into the centre of his own being. There is a great deal of Eastern philosophy and mysticism in the *Ancient Sage*, as, for instance, the feeling of the unity of all existence to the point of merging the personality into the universal.

But that one ripple on the boundless deep
Feels that the deep is boundless, and itself
For ever changing form, but evermore
One with the boundless motion of the deep.

We know that Tennyson had been studying the philosophy of Lâo-Tsze about this time; yet, though this is, as it were, grafted on to the poet's mind, still we may take it as being his genuine and deepest conviction. The nearest approach to a definite statement of it to be found in his poems is in the few stanzas called *The Higher Pantheism*, which he sent to be read at the first meeting of the Metaphysical Society in 1869.

> Speak to Him thou for He hears, and Spirit with Spirit can meet—
> Closer is He than breathing, and nearer than hands and feet.
>
> And the ear of man cannot hear, and the eye of man cannot see;
> But if we could see and hear, this Vision—were it not He?

In William Law, Burke, Coleridge, and Carlyle, we have a succession of great English prose-writers whose work and thought is permeated by a mystical philosophy. Of these four, Law is, during his later life, by far the most consistently and predominantly mystical. As has been indicated, there were many strains of influence which in the seventeenth century tended to foster mystical thought in England.

The group of Cambridge Platonists, to which Henry More belonged, gave new expression to the great Neoplatonic ideas, but in addition to this a strong vein of mysticism had been kept alive in Amsterdam, where the exiled Separatists had gone in 1593. They flourished there and waxed strong, and sent back to England during the next century a continual stream of opinion and literature. To this source can be traced the ideas which inspired alike the Quakers, the Seekers, the Behmenists, the Familists, and numberless other sects who all embodied a reaction against forms and ceremonies, which, in ceasing to be understood, had become lifeless.

These sects were, up to a certain point, mystical in thought, for they all believed in the "inner light," in the immediate revelation of God within the soul as the all-important experience. The persecutions of the Quakers under Charles II. tended to withdraw them from active philanthropy, and to throw them more in the direction of a personal and contemplative religion. It was then that the writings of Madame Bourignon, Madame Guyon, and Fénelon became popular, and were much read among a certain section of thinkers, while the influence of the teachings of Jacob Boehme, whose works had been translated into English between the years 1644 and 1692, can be traced, in diverse ways.

They impressed themselves on the thought of the founders of the Society of Friends, they produced a distinct "Behmenist" sect, and it would seem that the idea of the three laws of motion first reached Newton through his eager study of Boehme. But all this has nothing directly to do with literature, and would not concern us here were it not that in the eighteenth century William Law came into touch with many of these mystical thinkers, and that he has embodied in some of the finest prose in our language a portion of the "inspired cobbler's" vision of the universe. Law's character is one of considerable interest. Typically English, and in intellect typically of the eighteenth century, logical, sane, practical, he is not, at first sight, the man one would expect to find in sympathy with the mystics. Sincerity is the keynote of his whole nature, sincerity of thought, of belief, of speech, and of life. Sincerity implies courage, and Law was a brave man, never shirking the logical outcome of his convictions, from the day when he ruined his prospects at Cambridge, to the later years when he suffered his really considerable reputation to be eclipsed by his espousal of an uncomprehended and unpopular mysticism. He had a keen rather than a profound intellect, and his thought is lightened by brilliant flashes of wit or of grim satire. We can tell, however, from his letters and his later writings, that underneath a severe and slightly stiff exterior, were hidden emotion, enthusiasm, and great tenderness of feeling.

It is pertinent to note that middle life Law was well known as a most able and brilliant writer on most of the burning theological questions of the day, as well as the author of one of the best loved and most widely read practical and ethical treatises in the language, *A Serious Call to a Devout and Holy Life*. These earlier writings are by far the best known of his works, and it is with the *Serious Call* that his name will always be associated. Until middle age he showed no marked mystical tendency, although we know that from the time he was an undergraduate he was a "diligent reader" of mystical books, and that he had studied, among others, Dionysius the Areopagite, Ruysbroek, Tauler, Suso, and the seventeenth century Quietists, Fénelon, Madame Guyon, and Antoinette Bourignon.

When, however, he was about forty-six (c. 1733), he came across the writings of the seer who set his whole nature aglow with spiritual fervour, so that when he first read his works they put him into "a perfect sweat." Jacob Boehme—or Behmen, as he has usually been called in England—(1575-1624), the illiterate and untrained peasant shoemaker of Görlitz, is one of the most amazing phenomena in the history of mysticism, a history which does not lack wonders.

His work has so much influenced later mystical thought and philosophy that a little space must be devoted to him here. He lived outwardly the quiet, hard-working life of a simple German peasant, but inwardly—like his fellow-seer Blake—he lived in a glory of illumination, which by flashes revealed to him the mysteries and splendours he tries in broken and faltering words to record. He saw with the eye of his mind into the heart of things, and he wrote down as much of it as he could express. The older mystics—eastern and western alike—had laid stress on unity as seen in the nature of God and all things. No one more fully believed in ultimate unity than did Boehme, but he lays peculiar stress on the duality, or more accurately, the trinity in unity; and the central point of his philosophy is the fundamental postulate that all manifestation necessitates opposition. He asserted the uniformity of law throughout all existence, physical and spiritual, and this law, which applies all through nature, divine and human alike, is that nothing can reveal itself without resistance, good can only be known through evil, and weakness through strength, just as light is only visible when reflected by a dark body.

Thus when God, the Triune Principle, or *Will* under three aspects, desires to become manifest, He divides the Will into two, the "yes" and the "no," and so founds an eternal contrast to Himself out of His own hidden Nature, in order to enter into struggle with it, and finally to discipline and assimilate it. The object of all manifested nature is the transforming of the will which says "No" into the will which says "Yes," and this is brought about by seven organising spirits or forms. The first three of these bring nature out of the dark element to the point where contact with the light is possible. Boehme calls them harshness, attraction, and anguish, which in modern terms are contraction, expansion, and rotation. The first two are in deadly antagonism, and being forced into collision, form an endless whirl of movement. These two forces with their resultant effect are to be found all through manifested nature, within man and without, and are called by different names: good, evil and life, God, the devil and the world, homogeneity, heterogeneity, strain, or the three laws of motion, centripetal and centrifugal force, resulting in rotation. They are the outcome of the "nature" or "no" will, and are the basis of all manifestation. They are the "power" of God, apart from the "love," hence their conflict is terrible. When spirit and nature approach and meet, from the shock a new form is liberated, lightning or fire, which is the fourth moment or essence. With the lightning ends the development of the negative triad, and the evolution of the three higher forms then begins; Boehme calls them light or love, sound and substance; they are of the spirit, and in them contraction, expansion, and rotation are repeated in a new sense.

The first three forms give the stuff or strength of being, the last three manifest the quality of being good or bad, and evolution can proceed in either direction. The practical and ethical result of this living unity of nature is the side which most attracted Law, and it is one which is as simple to state as it is difficult to apply. Boehme's philosophy is one which can only be apprehended by living it.

Will, or desire, is the radical force in man as it is in nature and in the Godhead, and until that is turned towards the light, any purely historical or intellectual knowledge of these things is as useless as if hydrogen were to expect to become water by study of the qualities of oxygen, whereas what is needed is the actual union of the elements. The two most important of Law's mystical treatises are *An Appeal to all that Doubt*, 1740, and *The Way to Divine Knowledge*, 1752. The first of these should be read by any one desirous of knowing Law's later thought, for it is a clear and fine exposition of his attitude with regard more especially to the nature of man, the unity of all nature, and the quality of fire or desire.

The later book is really an account of the main principles of Boehme, with a warning as to the right way to apply them, and it was written as an introduction to the new edition of Boehme's works which Law contemplated publishing. The following is the aspect of Boehme's teaching which Law most consistently emphasises.

Man was made out of the Breath of God; his soul is a spark of the Deity. It therefore cannot die, for it "has the Unbeginning, Unending Life of God in it." Man has fallen from his high estate through ignorance and inexperience, through seeking separation, taking the part for the whole, desiring the knowledge of good and evil as separate things. The assertion of self is thus the root of all evil; for as soon as the will of man "turns to itself, and would, as it were, have a Sound of its own, it breaks off from the divine harmony, and falls into the misery of its own discord." For it is the state of our will that makes the state of our life.

Hence, by the "fall," man's standpoint has been dislocated from centre to circumference, and he lives in a false imagination.

Every quality is equally good, for there is nothing evil in God from whom all comes; but evil appears to be through separation. Thus strength and desire in the divine nature are necessary and magnificent qualities, but when, as in the creature, they are separated from love, they appear as evil. The analogy of the fruit is, in this connection a favourite one with both Law and Boehme. When a fruit is unripe (i.e. incomplete) it is sour, bitter, astringent, unwholesome; but when it has been longer exposed to the sun and air it becomes sweet, luscious, and good to eat.

Yet it is the same fruit, and the astringent qualities are not lost or destroyed, but transmuted and enriched, and are thus the main cause of its goodness. The only way to pass from this condition of "bitterness" to ripeness, from this false imagination to the true one, is the way of death. We must die to what we are before we can be born anew; we must die to the things of this world to which we cling, and for which we desire and hope, and we must turn towards God.

This should be the daily, hourly exercise of the mind, until the whole turn and bent of our spirit "points as constantly to God as the needle touched with the loadstone does to the north." To be alive in God, before you are dead to your own nature, is "a thing as impossible in itself, as for a grain of wheat to be alive before it dies." The root of all, then, is the will or desire. This realisation of the momentous quality of the will is the secret of every religious mystic, the hunger of the soul, as Law calls it, is the first necessity, and all else will follow. It is the seed of everything that can grow in us; "it is the only workman in nature, and everything is its work;" it is the true magic power. And this will or desire is always active; every man's life is a continual state of prayer, and if we are not praying for the things of God, we are praying for *something else*. For prayer is but the desire of the soul. Our imaginations and desires are, therefore, the greatest realities we have, and we should look closely to what they are. It is essential to the understanding of Law, as of Boehme, to remember his belief in the reality and actuality of the oneness of nature and of law. Nature is God's great Book of Revelation, for it is nothing else but God's own outward manifestation of what He inwardly is, and can do.... The mysteries of religion, therefore, are no higher, nor deeper than the mysteries of nature. God Himself is subject to this law.

There is no question of God's mercy or of His wrath, for it is an eternal principle that we can only receive what we are capable of receiving; and to ask why one person gains no help from the mercy and goodness of God while another does gain help is "like asking why the refreshing dew of heaven does not do that to the flint which it does to the vegetable plant." Self-denial, or mortification of the flesh is not a thing imposed upon us by the mere will of God: considered in themselves they have nothing of goodness or holiness, but they have their ground and reason in the nature of the thing, and are as "absolutely necessary to make way for the new birth, as the death of the husk and gross part of the grain is necessary to make way for its vegetable life."

These views are clear enough, but the more mystical ones, such as those which Law and Boehme held, for instance, about fire, can only be understood in the light of this living unity throughout nature, humanity, and divinity.

> "Everything in temporal Nature," says Law, "is descended out of that which is eternal, and stands as a palpable, visible Outbirth of it: ... Fire and Light and Air in this World are not only a true Resemblance of the Holy Trinity in Unity, but are the Trinity itself in its most outward, lowest kind of Existence or Manifestation.... Fire compacted,

created, separated from Light and Air, is the Elemental Fire of this World: Fire uncreated, uncompacted, unseparated from Light and Air, is the heavenly Fire of Eternity: Fire kindled in any material Thing is only Fire breaking out of its created, compacted state; it is nothing else but the awakening the Spiritual Properties of that Thing, which being thus stirred up, strive to get rid of that material Creation under which they are imprisoned ... and were not these spiritual Properties imprisoned in Matter, no material Thing could be made to burn.... Fire is not, cannot be a material Thing, it only makes itself visible and sensible by the Destruction of Matter." "If you ask what Fire is in its first true and unbeginning State, not yet entered into any Creature, It is the Power and Strength, the Glory and Majesty of eternal Nature.... If you ask what Fire is in its own spiritual Nature, it is merely a *Desire*, and has no other Nature than that of a *working Desire*, which is continually its *own Kindler*."

All life is a kindled fire in a variety of states, and every dead, insensitive thing is only dead because its fire is quenched or compressed, as in the case of a flint, which is in a state of death "because its fire is bound, compacted, shut up and imprisoned," but a steel struck against it, shows that every particle of the flint consists of this compacted fire.

But even as, throughout all nature, a state of death is an imprisoned fire, so throughout all nature is there only one way of kindling life. You might as well write the word "flame" on the outside of a flint and expect it to emit sparks as to imagine that any speculations of your reason will kindle divine life in your soul.

No; Would you have Fire from a Flint; its House of Death must be shaken, and its Chains of Darkness broken off by the Strokes of a Steel upon it. This must of all Necessity be done to your Soul, its imprisoned Fire must be awakened by the sharp Strokes of Steel, or no true Light of Life can arise in it.

If this mystical view of Fire be clear, it will be easy enough to follow what Law says about Light and Darkness, or Air, Water, and Earth, interpreting them all in the same way as "eternal Things become gross, finite, measurable, divisible, and transitory."

The Spirit of Prayer is of all Law's works the one most steeped in mystic ardour, and it possesses a charm, a melody of rhythm, and an imaginative quality rarely to be found in his earlier work. It should be read by those who would see Law under a little known aspect, and who do not realise that we have an English mystic who expresses, with a strength and beauty which Plotinus himself has rarely surpassed, the longing of the soul for union with the Divine.

Burke, Coleridge, and Carlyle are three very different writers who are alike in the mystical foundations of their belief, and who, through their writings, for over a hundred years in England carry on the mystical attitude and diffuse much mystical thought.

Burke, the greatest and most philosophic of English statesmen, was so largely because of his mystic spirit and imagination. Much of the greatness of his political pamphlets and speeches and of their enduring value is owing to the fact that his arguments are based on a sense of oneness and continuity, of oneness in the social organism and of continuity in the spirit which animates it. He believes in a life in the Universe, in a divine order, mysterious and inscrutable in origins and in ends, of which man and society are a part. This society is linked together in mutual service from the lowest to the highest. "Society is indeed a contract," he says in a memorable passage,

> It is a partnership in all science; a partnership in all art; a partnership in every virtue, and in all

> perfection. As the ends of such a partnership cannot be obtained in many generations, it becomes a partnership not only between those who are living, but between those who are living, those who are dead, and those who are to be born. Each contract of each particular state is but a clause in the great primæval contract of eternal society, linking the lower with the higher natures, connecting the visible and invisible world, according to a fixed compact sanctioned by the inviolable oath which holds all physical and all moral natures, each in their appointed place.

These are strange words for an English statesman to address to the English public in the year 1790; the thought they embody seems more in keeping with its surroundings when we hear it thundered out anew forty years later by the raw Scotch preacher-philosopher in the chapter he calls "Organic Filaments" in his odd but strangely stirring mystical rhapsody, *Sartor Resartus*.

In fact, it is on this belief of oneness, this interrelationship and interdependence that all Burke's deepest practical wisdom is based. It is on this he makes his appeal for high principle and noble example to the great families with hereditary trusts and fortunes, who, he says, he looks on as the great oaks that shade a country and perpetuate their benefits from generation to generation. This imaginative belief in the reality of a central spiritual life is always accompanied, whether definitely expressed or not, with a belief in the value of particulars, of the individual, as opposed to general statements and abstract philosophy. The mystic, who believes in an inward moulding spirit, necessarily believes that all reforms must come from within, and that, as Burke points out in the *Present Discontents*, good government depends not upon laws but upon individuals. Blake, in a characteristic phrase, says: "He who would do good to another must do it in minute particulars; general good is the plea of the hypocrite, flatterer, and scoundrel."

This sums up the essence of the social philosophy of these three thinkers, as seen by Burke's insistence on the value of concrete details in Coleridge's use of them in his Lay Sermon, and in Carlyle's belief in the importance of the single individual life in history. It is easy to see that Coleridge's attitude of mind and the main lines of his philosophy were mystical. From early years, as we know from Lamb, he was steeped in the writings of the Neo-platonists and these, together with Boehme, in whom he was much interested, and Schelling, strengthened a type of belief already natural to him. In spite of his devotion to the doctrines of Hartley, it is clear from his poetry and letters, that Coleridge very early had doubts concerning the adequacy of the intellect as an instrument for arriving at truth, and that at the same time the conviction was slowly gaining ground with him that an act of the will is necessary in order to bring man into contact with reality. Coleridge believed in a Spirit of the universe with which man could come into contact, both directly by desire, and also mediately through the forms and images of nature, and in the *Religious Musings* (1794) we get very early a statement of this mystical belief.

> There is one Mind, one omnipresent Mind
> Omnific. His most holy name is Love.
> From Him—
> ... we roam unconscious, or with hearts
> Unfeeling of our universal Sire,

and the greatest thing we can achieve, "our noon-tide majesty," is—

> to know ourselves
> Parts and proportions of one wonderous whole!

The way to attain this knowledge is not by a process of reasoning, but by a definite act of will, when the "drowséd soul" begins to feel dim recollections of its nobler nature, and so gradually becomes attracted and absorbed to perfect love—

and centered there
God only to behold, and know, and feel,
Till by exclusive consciousness of God
All self-annihilated it shall make
God its Identity: God all in all!

This sense of "oneness," with the desire to reach out to it, was very strong with Coleridge in these earlier years, and he writes to Thelwall in 1797, "The universe itself, what but an immense heap of little things?... My mind feels as if it ached to behold and know something *great*, something *one* and *indivisible*." He is ever conscious of the symbolic quality of all things by which we are visibly surrounded,

all that meets the bodily sense I deem
Symbolical, one mighty alphabet
For infant minds.

To pierce through the outer covering, and realise the truth which they embody, it is necessary to feel as well as to see, and it is the loss of this power of feeling which Coleridge deplores in those bitterly sad lines in the *Dejection Ode* when he gazes "with how blank an eye" at the starry heavens, and cries,

I see, not feel, how beautiful they are!

It is in this Ode that we find the most complete description in English verse of that particular state of depression and stagnation which often follows on great exaltation, and to which the religious mystics have given the name of the "dark night of the soul." This is an experience, not common to all mystics, but very marked in some, who, like St John of the Cross and Madame Guyon, are intensely devotional and ecstatic. It seems to be a well-defined condition of listlessness, apathy, and *dryness*, as they call it, not a state of active pain, but of terrible inertia, weariness, and incapacity for feeling; "a wan and heartless mood," says Coleridge,

A grief without a pang, void, dark, and drear,
A stifled, drowsy, unimpassioned grief,
Which finds no natural outlet, no relief,
In word, or sigh, or tear.

Coleridge's distrust of the intellect as sole guide, and his belief in some kind of intuitional act being necessary to the apprehension of reality, which he felt as early as 1794, was strengthened by his study of the German transcendental philosophers, and in March 1801 he writes, "My opinion is that deep thinking is attainable only by a man of deep feeling; and that all truth is a species of Revelation."

Coleridge, following Kant, gave the somewhat misleading name of "reason" (as opposed to "understanding") to the intuitive power by which man apprehends God directly, and, in his view, imagination is the faculty, which in the light of this intuitive reason interprets and unifies the symbols of the natural world. Hence its value, for it alone gives man the key

Of that eternal language, which thy God
Utters, who from eternity doth teach
Himself in all, and all things in himself.

Carlyle's mysticism is the essence of his being, it flames through his amazing medley of writings, it guides his studies and his choice of subjects, it unifies and explains his visions, his thought, and his doctrines. His is a mystical attitude and belief of a perfectly simple and broad kind, including no abstruse subtleties of metaphysical speculation, as with Coleridge, but based on one or two deeply rooted convictions. This position seems to have been reached by him partly through intellectual conflict which found relief and satisfaction in the view of life taken by Goethe, Fichte, and other German "transcendental" thinkers; but partly also through a definite psychical experience which befell him in Edinburgh when he was twenty-six, and which from that day changed for him the whole of his outlook on life. He speaks of it himself as "a Spiritual New-birth, or Baphometic Fire-baptism."

It came to him after a period of great wretchedness, of torture with doubt and despair, and—what is significant—"during three weeks of total sleeplessness." These are conditions which would be likely to reduce his body to the state of weakness and sensitiveness which seems often antecedent to psychic experience. He has given an account of the incident in *Sartor* (Book ii. chap, vii.), when, he says, "there rushed like a stream of fire over my whole soul; and I shook base Fear away from me for ever. I was strong, of unknown strength; a spirit, almost a god." The revelation seems to have been of the nature of a certainty and assertion of his own inherent divinity, his "native God-created majesty," freedom and potential greatness. This brought with it a characteristic defiance of untoward outer circumstances which gave him strength and resolution. "Perhaps," he says, "I directly thereupon began to be a man."

Carlyle believes that the world and everything in it is the expression of one great indivisible Force; that nothing is separate, nothing is dead or lost, but that all "is borne forward on the bottomless shoreless flood of Action, and lives through perpetual metamorphoses." Everything in the world is an embodiment of this great Force, this "Divine Idea," hence everything is important and charged with meaning. "Rightly viewed no meanest object is insignificant; all objects are as windows, through which the philosophic eye looks into Infinitude itself."

The universe is thus the "living visible garment of God," and "matter exists only spiritually," "to represent some Idea, and *body* it forth." We, each of us, are therefore one expression of this central spirit, the only abiding Reality; and so, in turn, everything we know and see is but an envelope or clothing encasing something more vital which is invisible within. Just as books are the most miraculous things men can make, because a book "is the *purest* embodiment a Thought of man can have," so great men are the highest embodiment of Divine Thought visible to us here. Great men are, as it were, separate phrases, "inspired texts" of the great book of revelation, perpetually interpreting and unfolding in various ways the Godlike to man (*Hero as Man of Letters*, and *Sartor*, Book ii. chap. viii.).

From this ground-belief spring all Carlyle's views and aims. Hence his gospel of hero-worship, for the "hero" is the greatest embodied "Idea" a man can know, he is a "living light fountain," he is "a man sent hither to make the divine mystery more impressively known to us." Hence it is clear that the first condition of the great man is that he should be sincere, that he should *believe*. "The merit of originality is not novelty: it is sincerity. The believing man is the original man." It is equally necessary that his admirers should be sincere, they too must believe, and not only, as Coleridge puts it, "believe that they believe." No more immoral act can be done by a human creature, says Carlyle, than to pretend to believe and worship when he does not.

9
The Mysticism of John Muir

> I do not understand the request of Moses, 'Show me thy glory,' but if he were here . . . after allowing him time to drink the glories of flower, mountain, and sky I would ask him how they compared with those of the Valley of the Nile . . . and I would inquire how he had the conscience to ask for more glory when such oceans and atmospheres were about him. King David was a better observer: 'The whole earth is full of thy glory.'
>
> —*John Muir*

A noted mystic writer John Muir was a Scottish-born American naturalist, author, and early advocate of preservation of wilderness in the United States. His letters, essays, and books telling of his adventures in nature, especially in the Sierra Nevada mountains of California, have been read by millions. His activism helped to save the Yosemite Valley, Sequoia National Park and other wilderness areas. The Sierra Club, which he founded, is now one of the most important conservation organizations in the United States. One of the most well-known hiking trails in the U.S., the 211-mile John Muir Trail, was named in his honor. Other places named in his honor are Muir Woods National Monument, Muir Beach, John Muir College, Camp Muir and Muir Glacier.

Hailed from Dunbar, East Lothian, Scotlandm his

parents were Daniel Muir and Ann Gilrye. He was the third of eight children: Margaret, Sarah, David, Daniel, Ann and Mary (twins), and the American-born Joanna. In his autobiography, he described his boyhood pursuits, which included fighting, either by re-enacting romantic battles of Scottish history or just scrapping on the playground, and hunting for birds' nests. Author Amy Marquis notes that he began his "love affair" with nature while young, and implies that it may have been in reaction to his strict religious upbringing. "His father believed that anything that distracted from Bible studies was frivolous and punishable." But the young Muir was a "restless spirit" and especially "prone to lashings." In 1849, Muir's family emigrated to the United States, starting a farm near Portage, Wisconsin called Fountain Lake Farm.

It has been designated a National Historic Landmark. Stephen Fox recounts that Muir's father found the Church of Scotland insufficiently strict in faith and practice, leading to their emigration and joining a congregation of the Campbellite Restoration Movement. By age 11, young Muir had learned to recite "by heart and by sore flesh" all of the New Testament and most of the Old Testament. But in maturity, Muir may have changed his orthodox beliefs. In a letter to his fond friend Emily Pelton, dated 23 May 1865, he wrote, "I never tried to abandon creeds or code of civilization; they went away of their own accord... without leaving any consciousness of loss." Elsewhere in his writings, he described the conventional image of a Creator, "as purely a manufactured article as any puppet of a half-penny theater."

At age 22, Muir enrolled at the University of Wisconsin–Madison, paying his own way for several years. There, under a towering black locust tree beside North Hall, Muir took his first botany lesson. A fellow student plucked a flower from the tree and used it to explain how the grand locust is a member of the pea family, related to the straggling pea plant. Fifty years later, the naturalist Muir described the day in his autobiography. "This fine lesson charmed me and sent me flying to the woods and meadows in wild enthusiasm." Muir took an eclectic approach to his studies, attending classes for two years but never being listed higher than a first year student due to his unusual selection of courses. Records showed his class status as "irregular gent" and, even though he never graduated, he learned enough geology and botany to inform his later wanderings.

Major Works

- *Studies in the Sierra* (1950 reprint of serials from 1874)
- *Picturesque California* (1888–1890)
- *The Mountains of California* (1894)
- *Our National Parks* (1901)
- *Stickeen*
- *Stickeen: An Adventure with a Dog and a Glacier* (1915)
- *Stickeen: The Story of a Dog* (1909)
- *My First Summer in the Sierra* (1911)
- *Edward Henry Harriman* (1911)
- *The Yosemite* (1912)
- *The Story of My Boyhood and Youth* (1913)
- *Letters to a Friend* (1915)
- *Travels in Alaska* (1915)
- *A Thousand-Mile Walk to the Gulf* (1916)
- *The Cruise of the Corwin* (1917)
- *Steep Trails* (1919)

In his later life, Muir devoted most of his time to the preservation of the Western forests. He petitioned the U.S. Congress for the National Park Bill that was passed in 1899, establishing both Yosemite and Sequoia National Parks. Because of the spiritual quality and enthusiasm toward nature expressed in his writings, he was able to inspire readers, including presidents and congressmen, to take action to help preserve large nature areas. He is today referred to as the "Father of the National Parks," and the

National Parks Service produced a short documentary on his life.

Steven Holmes, states that Muir has become "one of the patron saints of twentieth-century American environmental activity," both political and recreational. As a result, his writings are commonly discussed in books and journals, and he is often quoted in books by nature photographers such as Ansel Adams. "Muir has profoundly shaped the very categories through which Americans understand and envision their relationships with the natural world," writes Holmes. Muir was noted for being an ecological thinker, political spokesman, and religious prophet, whose writings became a personal guide into nature for countless individuals, making his name "almost ubiquitous" in the modern environmental consciousness. According William Anderson, Muir exemplified "the archetype of our oneness with the earth." In 1864, Muir left school to go to Canada, spending the spring, summer, and fall wandering the woods and swamps around Lake Huron collecting plants. With his money running out and winter coming, he met his brother Daniel in Ontario, where the two worked at a sawmill on the shore of Lake Huron until the summer of 1865. Muir's trip to Canada was likely influenced by the Civil War draft. By 1864, President Lincoln was calling up another half million soldiers, and Muir's chances of getting drafted were becoming increasingly likely.

Roderick Nash has described Muir's travels in Canada as journeys into wilderness to avoid military service, while Linnie Marsh Wolfe wrote that Muir decided that if he were not drafted, he "would wander a while" in the Canadian wilderness. Muir worked at the mill until it burned down in March 1866, and returned to the United States to work as an industrial engineer in Indianapolis. He proved valuable to his employers because of his inventiveness in improving the machines, processes, and lives of the laborers at a plant that manufactured carriage parts. In early March 1867, an accident changed the course of his life: a tool he was using slipped and struck him in the eye. He was confined to a darkened room for six weeks, worried if he'd ever regain his sight. When he did, "he saw the world—and his purpose—in a new light," writes Marquis.

Muir later wrote, "This affliction has driven me to the sweet fields. God has to nearly kill us sometimes, to teach us lessons." From that point on, he determined to "be true to myself" and follow his dream of exploration and study of plants. In September 1867, Muir undertook a walk of about 1,000 miles (1,600 km) from Indiana to Florida, which he recounted in his book *A Thousand-Mile Walk to the Gulf*. He had no specific route chosen, except to go by the "wildest, leafiest, and least trodden way I could find." Upon reaching Florida, he hoped to board a ship to South America and continue his wandering there. After contracting malaria on Florida's Gulf Coast, he abandoned his plans for South America. Instead, he sailed to New York and booked passage to California.

A Great Explorer of Nature

Muir immediately left for a week-long visit to Yosemite in 1868, a place he had only read about. Seeing it for the first time, Marquis notes that "he was overwhelmed by the landscape, scrambling down steep cliff faces to get a closer look at the waterfalls, whooping and howling at the vistas, jumping tirelessly from flower to flower." "We are now in the mountains and they are in us, kindling enthusiasm, making every nerve quiver, filling every pore and cell of us," Muir later wrote. . . . "No temple made with hands can compare with Yosemite... The grandest of all special temples of Nature." He later returned to Yosemite and worked as a shepherd for a season. He climbed a number of mountains, including Cathedral Peak, Mount Dana and hiked the old Indian trail down Bloody Canyon to Mono Lake. A gifted inventor, Muir designed a water-powered mill to cut wind-felled trees and he built a small cabin along Yosemite Creek, designing it so that a section of the stream would flow through a corner of the room, where he could enjoy the sound of running water. He lived in the cabin for two years, and wrote about this period in his book *First Summer in the Sierra* (1911).

During these years in Yosemite, Muir was unmarried, often unemployed, with no prospects for a career, and had "periods of anguish," writes naturalist author John Tallmadge. He was sustained by not only the natural environment, but also by reading the essays of naturalist author Ralph Waldo Emerson, who wrote about the very life that Muir was then living. On excursions into the back country of Yosemite, he traveled alone, carrying "only a tin cup, a handful of tea, a loaf of bread, and a copy of Emerson." He usually spent his evenings sitting by a campfire in his overcoat, reading Emerson under the stars. As the years passed, he became a "fixture in the valley," respected for his knowledge of natural history, his skill as a guide, and his vivid storytelling. Visitors to the valley often included scientists, artists, and celebrities, many of whom made a point of meeting with Muir.

Remarkably 1871, after Muir had lived in Yosemite for three years, Emerson, with a number of academic friends from Boston, arrived in Yosemite during a tour of the Western United States. The two men met, and according to Tallmadge, "Emerson was delighted to find at the end of his career the prophet-naturalist he had called for so long ago. . . And for Muir, Emerson's visit came like a laying on of hands."

Pursuit of his love of science, especially geology, often occupied his free time. Muir soon became convinced that glaciers had sculpted many of the features of the valley and surrounding area. This notion was in stark contradiction to the accepted contemporary theory, promulgated by Josiah Whitney (head of the California Geological Survey), which attributed the formation of the valley to a catastrophic earthquake. As Muir's ideas spread, Whitney would try to discredit Muir by branding him as an amateur. But Louis Agassiz, the premier geologist of the day, saw merit in Muir's ideas, and lauded him as "the first man I have ever found who has any adequate conception of glacial action."

In 1871, Muir discovered an active alpine glacier below Merced Peak, which helped his theories gain acceptance. He was a highly productive writer and had many of his accounts and papers published as far away as New York. Muir's former professor at the University of Wisconsin, Ezra Carr, and his wife Jeanne, encouraged Muir to put his ideas into print. They also introduced Muir to notables such as Emerson, as well as leading scientists such as Louis Agassiz, John Tyndall, John Torrey, Clinton Hart Merriam, and Joseph LeConte.

In addition to his geologic studies, Muir also investigated the plant life of the Yosemite area. In 1873 and 1874, he made field studies along the western flank of the Sierra on the distribution and ecology of isolated groves of Giant Sequoia. In 1876, the American Association for the Advancement of Science published Muir's paper on the subject. In the introduction, he explained his purpose: "During the past summer I explored the Sequoia belt of the Sierra Nevada, tracing its boundaries and learning what I could of the post-glacial history of the species, and of its future prospects. . . . Some of the answers obtained to these questions, seem plain and full of significance, and cannot I think, fail to interest every student of natural history."

In 1888 after seven years of managing the ranch, his health began to suffer. With his wife's prompting he returned to the hills to recover, climbing Mt. Rainier in Washington and writing *Ascent of Mount Rainier*. Muir travelled with the party that landed on Wrangel Island on the USS Corwin and claimed that island for the United States in 1881. He documented this experience in his book *The Cruise of the Corwin*.

Activism

A great activist, Muir threw himself into the preservationist role with great vigor. He envisioned the Yosemite area and the Sierra as pristine lands. He saw the greatest threat to the Yosemite area and the Sierra to be livestock, especially domestic sheep, calling them "hoofed locusts." In June 1889, the influential associate editor of *Century* magazine, Robert Underwood Johnson, camped with Muir in Tuolumne Meadows and saw firsthand the damage a large flock of sheep had done to the grassland. Johnson agreed to publish any article Muir wrote on the subject of excluding livestock from the Sierra high country.

He also agreed to use his influence to introduce a bill to Congress to make the Yosemite area into a national park, modeled after Yellowstone National Park. On 30 September 1890, the U.S. Congress passed a bill that essentially followed recommendations that Muir had suggested in two *Century* articles, *The Treasure of the Yosemite* and *Features of the Proposed National Park*, both published in 1890. But to Muir's dismay, the bill left Yosemite Valley under state control, as it had been since the 1860s. In early 1892, Professor Henry Senger, a philologist at the University of California, Berkeley contacted Muir with the idea of forming a local 'alpine club' for mountain lovers. Senger and San Francisco attorney Warren Olney sent out invitations "for the purpose of forming a 'Sierra Club.' Mr. John Muir will preside." On May 28, 1892, the first meeting of the Sierra Club was held to write articles of incorporation. One week later Muir was elected president, Olney vice-president, and a board of directors was chosen that included David Starr Jordan, president of the new Stanford University. Muir would remain president until his death 22 years later.

The Sierra Club immediately opposed efforts to reduce Yosemite National Park by half, and began holding educational and scientific meetings. One meeting in the fall of 1895 that included Muir, Joseph LeConte, and William

R. Dudley discussed the idea of establishing 'national forest reservations', which would later be called National Forests. The Sierra Club was active in the successful campaign to transfer Yosemite National Park from state to federal control in 1906. The fight to preserve Hetch Hetchy Valley was also taken up by the Sierra Club, with some prominent San Francisco members opposing the fight. Eventually a vote was held that overwhelmingly put the Sierra Club behind the opposition to Hetch Hetchy Dam.

In July 1896, Muir became associated with Gifford Pinchot, a national leader in the conservation movement. Pinchot was the first head of the United States Forest Service and a leading spokesman for the sustainable use of natural resources for the benefit of the people. His views eventually clashed with Muir and highlighted two diverging views of the use of the country's natural resources. Pinchot saw conservation as a means of managing the nation's natural resources for long-term sustainable commercial use. As a professional forester, his view was that "forestry is tree farming," without destroying the long-term viability of the forests. Muir valued nature for its spiritual and transcendental qualities. In one essay about the National Parks, he referred to them as "places for rest, inspiration, and prayers." He often encouraged city dwellers to experience nature for its spiritual nourishment. Both men opposed reckless exploitation of natural resources, including clear-cutting of forests. Even Muir acknowledged the need for timber and the forests to provide it, but Pinchot's view of wilderness management was far more utilitarian.

Their friendship ended late in the summer of 1897 when Pinchot released a statement to a Seattle newspaper supporting sheep grazing in forest reserves. Muir confronted Pinchot and demanded an explanation. When Pinchot reiterated his position, Muir told him: "I don't want any thing more to do with you." This philosophical divide soon expanded and split the conservation movement into two camps: the preservationists, led by Muir, and Pinchot's camp, who co-opted the term "conservation." The two men debated their positions in popular magazines, such as *Outlook*, *Harper's Weekly*, *Atlantic Monthly*, *World's Work*, and *Century*. Their contrasting views were highlighted again when the United States was deciding whether to dam Hetch Hetchy Valley. Pinchot favored the damming of the valley as "the highest possible use which could be made of it." In contrast, Muir proclaimed, "Dam Hetch Hetchy! As well dam for water-tanks the people's cathedrals and churches, for no holier temple has ever been consecrated by the hearts of man."

In 1903, President Theodore Roosevelt accompanied Muir on a visit to Yosemite. Muir joined Roosevelt in Oakland, California for the train trip to Raymond. The presidential entourage then traveled by stagecoach into the park. While traveling to the park, Muir told the president about state mismanagement of the valley and rampant exploitation of the valley's resources. Even before they entered the park, he was able to convince Roosevelt that the best way to protect the valley was through federal control and management.

After entering the park and seeing the magnificent splendor of the valley, the president asked Muir to show him the real Yosemite. Muir and Roosevelt set off largely by themselves and camped in the back country. The duo talked late into the night, slept in the brisk open air of Glacier Point, and were dusted by a fresh snowfall in the morning. It was a night Roosevelt would never forget. Muir then increased efforts by the Sierra Club to consolidate park management. In 1905 Congress transferred the Mariposa Grove and Yosemite Valley to the park.

Nature Writer

In his life, Muir published six volumes of writings, all describing explorations of natural settings. Four additional books were published posthumously. Several books were subsequently published that collected essays and articles from various sources. Miller writes that what was most important about his writings was not their quantity, but their "quality". He notes that they have had a "lasting effect on American culture in helping to create the desire and will to protect and preserve wild and natural environments."

His first appearance in print was by accident, writes Miller; a person he did not know submitted, without his permission or awareness, a personal letter to his friend Jeanne Carr, describing *Calypso borealis*, a rare flower he had encountered. The piece was published anonymously, identified as having been written by an "inspired pilgrim".Throughout his many years as a nature writer, Muir frequently rewrote and expanded on earlier writings from his journals, as well as articles published in magazines. He often compiled and organized such earlier writings as collections of essays or included them as part of narrative books.

After Muir returned to the United States, he spent the next four years exploring Yosemite, while at the same time writing articles for publication. During those years, Muir and Carr continued corresponding. She sent many of her friends to Yosemite to meet Muir and "to hear him preach the gospel of the mountains," writes Gisel. The most notable was naturalist and author Ralph Waldo Emerson. The importance of Carr, who continually gave Muir reassurance and inspiration, "cannot be overestimated," adds Gisel. It was "through his letters to her that he developed a voice and purpose." She also tried to promote Muir's writings by submitting his letters to a monthly magazine for publication. Muir came to trust Carr as his "spiritual mother," and they remained friends for 30 years. In one letter she wrote to Muir while he was living in Yosemite, she tried to keep him from despairing as to his purpose in life:

> I have often in my heart wondered what God was training you for. He gave you the eye within the

> eye, to see in all natural objects the realized ideas of His mind. He gave you pure tastes and the steady preference of whatsoever is most lovely and excellent. He has made you a more individualized existence than is common, and by your very nature and organization removed you from common temptations. . . . Dear friend, my recognition of you from the first was just this—"one of His beloved." When you are disposed to look hopelessly outward you may think, "Mrs. Carr believes fully in me. She would while there was enough left of my body to hold my soul." And you may think too that she does not pity half as much as she loves you.

The value of their friendship was first disclosed by a friend of Carr's, clergyman and writer G. Wharton James. After obtaining copies of their private letters from Carr, and despite pleadings from Muir to return them, he instead published articles about their friendship, using those letters as a primary source. In one such article, his focus was Muir's debt to Carr, stating that she was his "guiding star" who "led him into the noble paths of life, and then kept him there:"

We may beat about the bush all we will, but there is a spiritual potency in the love of a good, elderly woman for a young man that will stimulate him to his highest and best endeavors. Such was the relationship between these two, and John Muir is what he is today largely owing to the earlier impulses given to his soul by this highly intellectual and deeply spiritual woman.

Passion for Writing

Muir's friend, zoologist Henry Fairfield Osborn, writes that Muir's style of writing did not come to him easily, but only with intense effort. "Daily he rose at 4:30 o'clock, and after a simple cup of coffee labored incessantly . . . . he groans over his labors, he writes and rewrites and interpolates." Osborn notes that he preferred using the simplest English language, and therefore admired above all the writings of Carlyle, Emerson and Thoreau. "He is a very firm believer in Thoreau and starts by reading deeply of this author." His secretary, Marion Randall Parsons, also noted that "composition was always slow and laborious for him. . . . Each sentence, each phrase, each word, underwent his critical scrutiny, not once but twenty times before he was satisfied to let it stand." Muir would often say to her, "This business of writing books is a long, tiresome, endless job."

Miller speculates that Muir recycled his earlier writings partly due to his "dislike of the writing process." He adds that Muir "did not enjoy the work, finding it difficult and tedious." He was generally unsatisfied with the finished result, finding prose "a weak instrument for the reality he wished to convey." However, he was prodded by friends and his wife to keep writing and as a result of their influence he kept at it, although never satisfied. Muir wrote in 1872, "No amount of word-making will ever make a single soul to 'know' these mountains. One day's exposure to mountains is better than a cartload of books."

Remarkably, in one of his essays written in 1918, he gave an example of the deficiencies of writing versus experiencing nature:

> ...a tourist's frightened rush and scramble through the woods yields far less than the hunter's wildest stories, while in writing we can do but little more than to give a few names, as they come to mind, — beaver, squirrel, coon, fox, marten, fisher, otter, ermine, wildcat, — only this instead of full descriptions of the bright-eyed furry throng, their snug home nests, their fears and fights and loves, how they get their food, rear their young, escape their enemies, and keep themselves warm and well and exquisitely clean through all the pitiless weather.

On Nature and Theology

Muir understood that if he hoped to discover truth, he had to turn to what he believed to be the most accurate sources. In his book, *The Story of My Boyhood and Youth* (1913), he writes that during his childhood, his father made him read the Bible every day. Muir eventually memorized three quarters of the Old Testament and all of the New Testament. Historian Dennis Williams adds that his father had read Josephus's *War of the Jews* in order to understand the culture of first-century Palestine, as it was written by an eyewitness, and illuminated the culture during the period of the New Testament.

But as Muir became attached to the American natural landscapes he explored, Williams notes that he began to see another "primary source for understanding God: the Book of Nature." According to Williams, in nature, especially in the wilderness, Muir was able to study the plants and animals in an environment that he believed "came straight from the hand of God, uncorrupted by civilization and domestication." As Tallmadge notes, Muir's belief in this "Book of Nature" compelled him to tell the story of "this creation in words any reader could understand." As a result, his writings were to become "prophecy, for [they] sought to change our angle of vision."

Williams notes that Muir's philosophy and world view rotated around his perceived dichotomy between civilization and nature. From this developed his core belief that "wild is superior". His nature writings became a "synthesis of natural theology" with scripture that helped him understand the origins of the natural world. According to Williams, philosophers and theologians such as Thomas Dick suggested that the "best place to discover the true attributes of deity was in Nature." He came to believe that God was always active in the creation of life and thereby kept the natural order of the world. As a result, Muir "styled himself as a John the Baptist," adds Williams, "whose duty was to immerse in 'mountain baptism' everyone he could." Williams concludes that Muir saw nature as a great teacher, "revealing the mind of God," and this belief became the central theme of his later journeys and the "subtext" of his nature writing. During his career as writer and while living in the mountains, Muir continued to experience the "presence of the divine in nature," writes Holmes From *Travels in Alaska*: "Every particle of rock or water or air has God by its side leading it the way it should go; The clearest way into the Universe is through a forest wilderness; In God's wildness is the hope of the world." His personal letters also conveyed these feelings of ecstasy.

Catherine Albanese stated that in one of his letters, "Muir's eucharist made Thoreau's feast on wood-chuck and huckleberry seem almost anemic." She added that "Muir had successfully taken biblical language and inverted it to proclaim the passion of attachment, not to a supernatural world but to a natural one. To go to the mountains and sequoia forests, for Muir, was to engage in religious worship of utter seriousness and dedication." She quotes Muir's letter: Do behold the King in his glory, King Sequoia. Behold! Behold! seems all I can say. Some time ago I left all for Sequoia: have been and am at his feet fasting and praying for light, for is he not the greatest light in the woods; in the world.

Of Sensory Perceptions and Light

During his first summer in the Sierra as a shepherd, Muir wrote field notes that emphasized the role that the senses play in human perceptions of the environment. According to Williams, he speculated that the world was an unchanging entity that was interpreted by the brain through the senses, and, writes Muir, "If the creator were to bestow a new set of senses upon us . . . we would never doubt that we were in another world. . . " While doing his studies of nature, he would try to remember everything he observed as if his senses were recording the impressions, until he could write them in his journal. As a result of his intense desire to remember facts, he filled his field journals with notes on precipitation, temperature, and even cloud formations.

However, Muir took his journal entries further than recording factual observations. Williams notes that the observations he recorded amounted to a description of "the sublimity of Nature," and what amounted to "an aesthetic and spiritual notebook." Muir felt that his task was more than just recording "phenomena," but also to "illuminate the spiritual implications of those phenomena," writes Williams. For Muir, mountain skies, for example, seemed to be painted with light, and came to "symbolize divinity." He would often describe his observations in terms of light:

> ". . . . so gloriously colored, and so luminous, . . . awakening and warming all the mighty host to do gladly their shining day's work. . . to whose light everything seems equally divine, opening a thousand windows to show us God."

Muir biographer Steven Holmes notes that Muir used words like "glory" and "glorious" to suggest that light was taking on a religious dimension: "It is impossible to overestimate the importance of the notion of glory in Muir's published writings, where no other single image carries more emotional or religious weight," adding that his words "exactly parallels its Hebraic origins," in which biblical writings often indicate a divine presence with light, as in the burning bush or pillar of fire, and described as "the glory of God."

Nature as Home

Muir would often use the term "home" as a metaphor for both nature and his general attitude toward the "natural world itself," notes Holmes. He would often use domestic language to describe his scientific observations, as when he saw nature as providing a home for even the smallest plant life: "the little purple plant, tended by its Maker, closed its petals, crouched low in its crevice of a home, and enjoyed the storm in safety." Muir also saw nature as his own home, as when he wrote friends and described the Sierra as "God's mountain mansion." He considered not only the mountains as home, however, as he also felt a closeness even to the smallest objects: "The very stones seem talkative, sympathetic, brotherly. No wonder when we consider that we all have the same Father and Mother."

In his later years, he would use the metaphor of nature as home in his writings to promote wilderness preservation. In one of his essays aimed at the common person he wrote, "Thousands of tired, nerve-shaken, over-civilized people are beginning to find out that going to the mountains is going home; that wilderness is a necessity; and that mountain parks and reservations are useful not only as fountains of timber and irrigating rivers, but as fountains of life."

Not surprisingly, Muir's deep-seeted feeling about nature as being his true home led to tension with his family at his home in Martinez, California. He once told a visitor to his ranch there, "This is a good place to be housed in during stormy weather, . . . to write in, and to raise children in, but it is not my home. Up there," pointing towards the Sierra Nevada, "is my home."

John Muir died at California Hospital in Los Angeles on 24 December 1914 of pneumonia at age 76, after a brief visit to Daggett, California to see his daughter Helen Muir Funk.

In describing his first explorations of the Sierras, John Muir wrote, "Oh, these vast, calm measureless mountain days, inciting at once to work and rest! Days in whose light every thing seems equally divine, opening a thousand windows to show us God." It is probably safe to say that no American ever experienced wilderness as religious ecstasy more than Muir. He called the Sierras the Range of Light and — as Light in the sky — they evoked in him immense religious longings. Before the magnificence of nature, he found himself dumb with admiration, prostrate and humble before the power of the God who created it all. Muir declared himself willing to endure self-denial if that was the price of learning to read from the divine manuscript which was the rocks and the trees. All wilderness, he wrote, seems full of tricks and hidden plans to drive us up into God's light.

Of the Sierras he declared:

> These blessed mountains are so compactly filled with God's beauty, no petty personal hope or experience has room to be . . . . the whole body seems to feel beauty when exposed to it as it feels the campfire or sunshine, entering not by the eyes alone, but equally through all one's flesh like radiant heat, making a passionate ecstatic pleasure-glow not explainable. One's body then seems homogeneous throughout, sound as a crystal.

While sauntering through the mountains, he said he knew complete freedom. He had experiences that seemed timeles and spaceless. Occasionally, he felt his body had no weight. "Life seems neither long nor short," he once wrote, "and we take no more heed to save time or make haste than do the trees and stars." He experienced what he believed was God's time, an immense perspective which made the quick transformations of the cloud-mountains and the slow transformations of the granite mountain roughly equivalent. He entered the eternal now and experienced days that seemed to have neither end nor beginning. Muir claimed that in the Sierras he found a practical sort of immortality, and he at times experienced himself as dissolved into the landscape. The mountains, he said, are fountains, places where the transcendent spews out of the earth.

In the Range of Light, Muir experienced the interrelated of all things, the union of rocks and clouds, the humanness of the landscape, the wilderness in the human soul. He declared a kinship with the wild Nature he loved, a oneness.

Muir repeatedly compared Yosemite Valley and the mountain peaks around it to a church or a cathedral. After many awe- struck moments gazing at Cathedral Rock through openings in the trees, he decided to climb to the top. Writing of this experience, he said it was the first time since he had come to California that he had been to church. Atop this giant monolith, he had the sensation of doors opening, revealing the transcendent realm. On this mountain alter he found cassiope — a species of flower for which he had been searching. The bells of the flowers, he wrote, were ringing with the sweetest church music he had ever heard.

It puzzled Muir that many of his fellow humans did not appreciate God's grandeur as it manifested itself in the wilderness. His companion on his first summer in the Sierra, a shepherd named Billy — who, in Muir's descriptions, seems something of a Sancho Panza figure — called Yosemite Valley "a lot of rocks — a hole in the ground." Muir witnessed other tourists who seemed unimpresssed by the majesty of Yosemite: he saw fishermen baiting their hooks "in the holiest of temples ignoring God himself as he preaches sublime water and stone sermons."

All Muir's books seem to say the same thing over and over: "Look! Nature is overflowing with the grandeur of God!" To Muir religious feelings were as natural as breathing. Nature herself seemed constantly engaged in worship. Even trees bowing in the wind were celebrants of a primordial religion.

A few minutes ago every tree was excited, bowing to the roaring storm, waving, swirling, tossing their branches in glorious enthusiasm like worship. But though to the outer ear these trees are now silent, their songs never cease. Every hidden cell is throbbing with music and life, every fiber thrilling like harp strings, while incense is ever flowing from the balsam bells and leaves. No wonder the hills and groves were God's first temples, and the more they are cut down and hewn into cathedrals and churches, the farther off and dimmer seems the Lord himself.

Though Muir didn't worship the trees, he did seem to worship with the trees and through the trees. In his idiosyncratic and exuberant way he celebrated the mysteries. Just who the God was he celebrated is unclear. Much of the language sounds Christian and orthodox, but there is a Dionysian or pagan element that spills through it all. His strivings and his imagery are always upward towards what could, I think, be characterized as a Pure Land — an ideal world that lies in the clouds. "The region above our camp," he writes in *My First Summer in the Sierra*, "is still wild, and higher lies the snow about as trackless as the sky." As a hummingbird finds itself drawn to the flowers, so did John Muir find himself drawn to this Pure Land in the sky. Of one of his first ascents into the Sierras, he wrote, "Now away we go toward the topmost mountains. Many still, small voices, as well as the noon thunder, are calling, 'Come higher.'"

On coming to a high mountain meadow, he once remarked that not a single leaf or petal seems to be misplaced. This passage brings to mind the Zen aphorism that no snowflake ever falls in the wrong place. As far as Muir was concerned the deer walking through this meadow or the bears rolling around in it in no way spoiled it — their trampling was to him a gentle cultivation. On more than one occasion, Muir wrote of being struck by how clean nature is. All plants are clean; all animals are clean. Of all the living things on the planet, mankind alone seems dirty. Even the occasional Indians he passed in the wilderness struck him as being dirty. Muir considered the high mountains to be a mirror that reflects the Creator. When he was in the wilderness he sensed the entire world glowing with God's radiance.

Muir said the wildflowers he found at the top of one Sierra peak were "a cloud of witness to Nature's love in what we in our timid ignorance and unbelief call howling desert." Though the surface of the ground seemed, at first glance, to be dull and foreboding, a close inspection showed that it shined and sparkled with crystals: mica, hornblende, feldspars, quartz, tourmaline. This gave the mountaintop a radiance, which in some places was dazzling. To him every crystal and every flower was "a window opening into heaven, a mirror reflecting the Creator."

To Muir all human beings have spiritual strivings, and the wilderness is a natural place to consummate the longings of the soul. In the Sierras, Muir attained a wider existence:

We are now in the mountains and they arein us, kindling enthusiasm, making every nerve quiver, filling every pore and cell of us. Our flesh-and-bone tabernacle seems transparent as glass to the beauty about us, as if truly an inseparable part of it, thrilling with the air and trees, streams and rocks, in the waves of the sun, — a part of all nature, neither old nor young, sick nor well, but immortal. Just now I can hardly conceive of any bodily condition dependent on food or breath any more than the ground or the sky. How glorious a conversion, so complete and wholesome it is.

Muir called the mountains love-monuments. He elected to follow God in the way that came natural — by drifting across the mountains and down into the canyons like the shadow of a cloud, like a faithful servant to the divine winds.

REFERENCES

Adams, Ansel. *America's Wilderness: the Photographs of Ansel Adams, with the Writings of John Muir*, Philadelphia, PA: Courage Books, 2002

Anderson, William. *The Scottish Nation: Or. The Surnames, Families, Literature, Honours, and Biographical History of the People of Scotland*. London: A. Fullarton Co., 1877.

Colby, William (December, 1967). "The Story of the Sierra Club". *Sierra Club Bulletin*. Sierra Club.

Ehrlich, Gretel. *John Muir: Nature's Visionary*. Washington, D.C.: National Geographic Society, 2000.

Fleck, Richard F. (February 1978). "John Muir's Evolving Attitudes toward Native American Cultures". *American Indian Quarterly* (University of Nebraska Press) 4 (1): 19–31.

Fox, Stephen R. (1985). *The American conservation movement : John Muir and his legacy*. Univ of Wisconsin Press. p. 30.

Holmes, Steven. *The Young John Muir: An Environmental Biography*. Madison: Univ. of Wisconsin Press, 1999. p. 178.

John Muir (1917). "The Cruise of the Corwin". Boston and New York: Houghton Mifflin Company.

Marquis, Amy Leinbach. (Fall 2007.) "A Mountain Calling", *National Parks Magazine*, retrieved on 23 October 2009.

Miller, Barbara Kiely. *John Muir*, Gareth Stevens Publ. (2008) p. 10

Muir, John and Teale, Edwin Way. *The Wilderness World of John Muir*, Mariner Books (1954, 2001)

Wenk, Elizabeth, and Kathy Morey. *John Muir Trail: The Essential Guide to Hiking America's Most Famous Trail*. Berkeley, CA: Wilderness Press, 2007.

Wolfe, Linnie Marsh, *Son of the Wilderness: The Life of John Muir*, Alfred A. Knopf, 1945.

10

Metaphysics and Metaphysical Poetry

> "...though we cannot know these objects as things in themselves, we must yet be in a position at least to think them as things in themselves; otherwise we should be landed in the absurd conclusion that there can be appearance without anything that appears."
>
> — *Immanuel Kant, Critique of Pure Reason*

It is pertinent to note that 'Metaphysics ' is closely related with Mysticism in philosophic terms.

Here in this chapter first we shall elucidate methaphysics, because it is necessary to understand the methaphysical poetry in English at core. Then we will address the essence of metaphysical poetry.

'Metaphysics' is a branch of philosophy concerned with explaining the fundamental nature of being and the world although it is not easily defined. Traditionally, metaphysics attempts to answer two questions: "What is *there*?" and "What is it (that is, whatever it is that there is) *like*?"

Etymologically, word derives from the Greek words *metá,* meaning "beyond" or "after" and *physiká,* meaning "physical", "physical" referring to those works on matter by Aristotle in antiquity. The prefix *meta-* ("beyond") was attached to the chapters in Aristotle's work that followed after the chapters on "physics," in posthumously edited collections. Aristotle himself did not call these works Metaphysics. Aristotle called some of the subjects treated there "first philosophy." A central branch of metaphysics is ontology, the investigation into what types of things there are in the world and what relations these things bear to one another. The metaphysician also attempts to clarify the notions by which people understand the world, including existence, objecthood, property, space, time, causality, and possibility.

Before the development of modern science, scientific questions were addressed as a part of metaphysics known as "natural philosophy"; the term "science" itself meant "knowledge" of epistemological origin. The scientific method, however, made natural philosophy an empirical and experimental activity unlike the rest of philosophy, and by the end of the eighteenth century it had begun to be called "science" to distinguish it from philosophy. Thereafter, metaphysics became the philosophical enquiry of a non-empirical character into the nature of existence. The first known metaphysician, according to Aristotle, is Thales. His concept of *Arche* or the source, first principle, or substratum was that of moisture, which is frequently translated as "water." Other Miletians, such as Anaximander and Anaximenes, also had a monistic conception of Arche. For Thales, the cosmos had a harmonious structure, and thus was subject to rational understanding. Parmenides of Elea held that the multiplicity of existing things, their changing forms and motion, are but an appearance of a single eternal reality ("Being"), thus giving rise to the Parmenidean principle that "all is one".

From this concept of Being, he went on to say that all claims of change or of non-Being are illogical. Because he introduced the method of basing claims about appearances on a logical concept of Being, he is considered one of the founders of metaphysics.

In fact, Metaphysics was called the "first philosophy" by Aristotle. The editor of his works, Andronicus of Rhodes, is thought to have placed the books on first philosophy right after another work, *Physics*, and called them *ta meta ta physika biblia* or "the books that come after the [books on] physics". This was misread by Latin scholiasts, who thought it meant "the science of what is beyond the physical". In the English language, the word comes by way of the Medieval Latin *metaphysica*, the neuter plural of Medieval Greek *metaphysika*. While its Greek and Latin origins are clear, various dictionaries trace its first appearance in English to the mid-sixteenth century, although in some cases as early as 1387.

Aristotle's *Metaphysics* was divided into three parts, in addition to some smaller sections related to a philosophical lexicon and some reprinted extracts from the *Physics*, which are now regarded as the proper branches of traditional Western metaphysics:

Ontology

The study of Being and existence; includes the definition and classification of entities, physical or mental, the nature of their properties, and the nature of change.

Natural Theology

The study of a God or Gods; involves many topics, including among others the nature of religion and the world, existence of the divine, questions about Creation, and the numerous religious or spiritual issues that concern humankind in general.

Universal Science

In fact, the study of first principles, which Aristotle believed were the foundation of all other inquiries. An example of such a principle is the law of noncontradiction and the status it holds in non-paraconsistent logics. Universal science or first philosophy treats of "being qua being"—that is, what is basic to all science before one adds the particular details of any one science. Essentially "being *qua* being" may be translated as "being insofar as being goes" or as "being in terms of being." This includes topics such as causality, substance, species and elements, as well as the notions of relation, interaction, and finitude.

As such, Metaphysics as a discipline was a central part of academic inquiry and scholarly education even before the age of Aristotle, who considered it "the Queen of Sciences." Its issues were considered no less important than the other main formal subjects of physical science, medicine, mathematics, poetics and music.

Since the beginning of modern philosophy during the seventeenth century, problems that were not originally considered within the bounds of metaphysics have been added to its purview, while other problems considered metaphysical for centuries are now typically relegated to their own separate regions in philosophy, such as philosophy of religion, philosophy of mind, philosophy of perception, philosophy of language, and philosophy of science.

In some cases, subjects of metaphysical scholarship have been found to be entirely physical and natural, thus making them part of physics proper.

Main Themes

It is pertinent to note that most positions that can be taken with regards to any of the following questions are endorsed by one or another notable philosopher. It is often difficult to frame the questions in a non-controversial manner. Some philosophers endorse views according to which there are abstract objects such as numbers, or Universals. (Universals are properties that can be instantiated by multiple objects, such as redness or squareness.)

Abstract objects are generally regarded as being outside of space and time, and/or as being causally inert.

Mathematical objects and fictional entities and worlds are often given as examples of abstract objects.

The view that there really are no abstract objects is called nominalism. Realism about such objects is exemplified by Platonism. Other positions include moderate realism, as espoused by Aristotle, and conceptualism. Other positions such as formalism and fictionalism that do not attribute any existence to mathematical entities are anti-realist.

Cosmology and Cosmogony

Similarly, Cosmology is the branch of metaphysics that deals with the world as the totality of all phenomena in space and time. Historically, it has had quite a broad scope, and in many cases was founded in religion. The ancient Greeks did not draw a distinction between this use and their model for the cosmos.

However, in modern times it addresses questions about the Universe beyond the scope of physical science. It is distinguished from religious cosmology in that it approaches these questions using philosophical methods (e.g. dialectics). Cosmogony deals specifically with the origin of the universe.

Modern metaphysical cosmology and cosmogony try to address questions such as:

- What is the origin of the Universe? What is its first cause? Is its existence necessary?
- What are the ultimate material components of the Universe?
- What is the ultimate reason for the existence of the Universe? Does the cosmos have a purpose?

Determinism and Free Will

It is also significant to note that determinism is the philosophical proposition that every event, including human cognition, decision and action, is causally determined by an unbroken chain of prior occurrences. It holds that no random, spontaneous, mysterious, or miraculous events occur. The principal consequence of the deterministic claim is that it poses a challenge to the existence of free will. The problem of free will is the problem of whether rational agents exercise control over their own actions and decisions. Addressing this problem requires understanding the relation between freedom and causation, and determining whether the laws of nature are causally deterministic. Some philosophers, known as Incompatibilists, view determinism and free will as mutually exclusive.

If they believe in determinism, they will therefore believe free will to be an illusion, a position known as *Hard Determinism*. Proponents range from Baruch Spinoza to Ted Honderich. Others, labeled Compatibilists (or "Soft Determinists"), believe that the two ideas can be coherently reconciled. Adherents of this view include Thomas Hobbes and many modern philosophers. Incompatibilists who accept free will but reject determinism are called Libertarians, a term not to be confused with the political sense.

Robert Kane is a modern defender of this theory. It is believed that determinism necessarily entails that humanity or individual humans have no influence on the future and its events (a position known as Fatalism). Determinists believe a human being's future depends on present and past events beyond the individual's influence. Proponents of the Copenhagen Interpretation of quantum mechanics believe that Determinism was proven incorrect with the Heisenberg Uncertainty Principle, which states that certain corresponding physical quantities (such as position and momentum, energy and time, eigenstates of spin in non-parallel directions) cannot be determined simultaneously to an arbitrarily small error.

For example, the more precisely a particle's position is measured, the less precisely one can know its momentum from the same measurement. If the momentum is more precisely measured to account for this, the uncertainty in the position will rise. This counter-intuitive result is a consequence of the wave-like behavior of subatomic particles.

The Heisenberg Uncertainty Principle is thus a statement providing an inverse correlation between the uncertainties of certain corresponding measurements. This line of reasoning has led physicists to use the "wave function" to describe physical systems. While differential equations govern the evolution of the wave function, the wave function itself only specifies the probability of an event to be measured. Thus, while the evolution of the wave function is deterministic, the history of a particle is not. The widely held view amongst physicists regards the apparent determinism of Newtonian dynamics, for example, as the limiting behavior of inherently probabilistic phenomena.

Classical physics is then considered a convenient and sufficiently accurate description of nature only at macroscopic scales. A large enough scale is usually thought of as much larger than the Compton wavelength of the object considered. Alternative interpretations of quantum theory, such as de Broglie–Bohm theory and the many-worlds interpretation, provide a deterministic theoretical framework that is consistent with empirical observation of quantum mechanical phenomena. Notable physicists, such as Albert Einstein and Erwin Schrodinger, never believed that Quantum Mechanics was a fundamental theory. Einstein is famous for believing that while Quantum Mechanics provided good experimental predictions, it should ultimately be replaced with a deterministic theory that could account for the seemingly probabilistic nature of the atomic regime.

In a letter to Max Born, Einstein wrote, "Quantum mechanics is certainly imposing. But an inner voice tells me that it is not yet the real thing. The theory says a lot, but does not really bring us any closer to the secret of the 'old one'. I, at any rate, am convinced that *He* does not throw dice."

Identity and Change

The Greeks took some extreme positions on the nature of change: Parmenides denied that change occurs at all, while Heraclitus thought change was ubiquitous: "[Y]ou cannot step into the same river twice". Identity, sometimes called Numerical Identity, is the relation that a "thing" bears to itself, and which no "thing" bears to anything other than itself (cf. sameness). According to Leibniz, if some object *x* is identical to some object *y*, then any property that *x* has, *y* will have as well. However, it seems, too, that objects can change over time.

If one were to look at a tree one day, and the tree later lost a leaf, it would seem that one could still be looking at that same tree. Two rival theories to account for the relationship between change and identity are Perdurantism, which treats the tree as a series of tree-stages, and Endurantism, which maintains that the tree—the same tree—is present at every historical stage.

Mind and Matter

The nature of matter was a problem in its own right in early philosophy. Aristotle himself introduced the idea of matter in general to the Western world, adapting the term *hyle*, which originally meant "lumber." Early debates centered on identifying a single underlying principle. Water was claimed by Thales, air by Anaximenes, *Apeiron* (the Boundless) by Anaximander, fire by Heraclitus. Democritus, in conjunction with his mentor, Leucippus, conceived of an atomic theory many centuries before it was accepted by modern science.

It is worth noting, however, that the grounds necessary to ensure validity to the proposed theory's veridical nature were not scientific, but just as philosophical as those traditions espoused by Thales and Anaximander. The nature of the mind and its relation to the body has been seen as more of a problem as science has progressed in its mechanistic understanding of the brain and body. Proposed solutions often have ramifications about the nature of mind as a whole. René Descartes proposed substance dualism, a theory in which mind and body are essentially different, with the mind having some of the attributes traditionally assigned to the soul, in the seventeenth century. This creates a conceptual puzzle about how the two interact (which has received some strange answers, such as occasionalism).

Evidence of a close relationship between brain and mind, such as the Phineas Gage case, have made this form of dualism increasingly unpopular. Another proposal discussing the mind-body problem is idealism, in which the material is sweepingly eliminated in favor of the mental. Idealists, such as George Berkeley, claim that material objects do not exist unless perceived and only as perceptions. The "German idealists" such as Fichte, Hegel and Schopenhauer took Kant as their starting-point, although it is debatable how much of an idealist Kant himself was. Idealism is also a common theme in Eastern philosophy.

Related ideas are panpsychism and panexperientialism, which say everything *has* a mind rather than everything exists *in* a mind. Alfred North Whitehead was a twentieth-century exponent of this approach. Idealism is a monistic theory that holds there is a single universal substance or principles. Neutral monism, associated in different forms with Baruch Spinoza and Bertrand Russell, seeks to be less extreme than idealism, and to avoid the problems of substance dualism. It claims that existence consists of a single substance that in itself is neither mental nor physical, but is capable of mental and physical aspects or attributes – thus it implies a dual-aspect theory. For the last one hundred years, the dominant metaphysics has without a doubt been materialistic monism.

Type identity theory, token identity theory, functionalism, reductive physicalism, nonreductive physicalism, eliminative materialism, anomalous monism, property dualism, epiphenomenalism and emergence are just some of the candidates for a scientifically informed account of the mind.

Celebrated recent philosophers of mind include David Armstrong, Ned Block, David Chalmers, Patricia and Paul Churchland, Donald Davidson, Daniel Dennett, Douglas Hofstadter, Jerry Fodor, David Lewis, Thomas Nagel, Hilary Putnam, John Searle, John Smart, Ludwig Wittgenstein, and Fred Alan Wolf.

Necessity and Possibility

It is pertinent to note that Metaphysicians investigate questions about the ways the world could have been. David Lewis, in "On the Plurality of Worlds," endorsed a view called Concrete Modal realism, according to which facts about how things could have been are made true by other concrete worlds, just like ours, in which things are different. Other philosophers, such as Gottfried Leibniz, have dealt with the idea of possible worlds as well. The idea of necessity is that any necessary fact is true across all possible worlds; that is, we could not imagine it to be otherwise. A possible fact is true in some possible world, even if not in the actual world.

For example, it is possible that cats could have had two tails, or that any particular apple could have not existed. By contrast, certain propositions seem necessarily true, such as analytic propositions, e.g. "All bachelors are unmarried." The particular example of analytic truth being necessary is not universally held among philosophers. A less controversial view might be that self-identity is necessary, as it seems fundamentally incoherent to claim that for any *x*, it is not identical to itself; this is known as the *law of identity*, a putative "first principle".

Aristotle describes the *principle of non-contradiction*, "It is impossible that the same quality should both belong and not belong to the same thing . . . This is the most certain of all principles . . . Wherefore they who demonstrate refer to this as an ultimate opinion. For it is by nature the source of all the other axioms."

Objects and their Properties

The world seems to contain many individual things, both physical, like apples, and abstract such as love and the number 3; the former objects are called particulars. Particulars are said to have attributes, e.g. size, shape, color, location and two particulars may have some such attributes in common. Such attributes, are also termed Universals or Properties; the nature of these, and whether they have any real existence and if so of what kind, is a long-standing issue, realism and nominalism representing opposing views. Metaphysicians concerned with questions about universals or particulars are interested in the nature of objects and their properties, and the relationship between the two.

Some, e.g. Plato, argue that properties are abstract objects, existing outside of space and time, to which particular objects bear special relations. David Armstrong holds that universals exist in time and space but only at their instantiation and their discovery is a function of science. Others maintain that what particulars are is a bundle or collection of properties.

Religion and Spirituality

In fact, Theology is the study of a God or gods and the nature of the divine. Whether there is a god (monotheism), many gods (polytheism) or no gods (atheism), or whether it is unknown or unknowable whether any gods exist (agnosticism), and whether the Divine intervenes directly in the world (theism), or its sole function is to be the first cause of the universe (deism); these and whether a God or gods and the World are different (as in panentheism and dualism), or are identical (as in pantheism), are some of the primary metaphysical questions concerning philosophy of religion. Within the standard Western philosophical tradition, theology reached its peak under the medieval school of thought known as scholasticism, which focused primarily on the metaphysical aspects of Christianity.

The work of the scholastics is still an integral part of modern philosophy, with key figures such as Thomas Aquinas still playing an important role in the philosophy of religion. In Book XI of the Confessions, Saint Augustine of Hippo asked the fundamental question about the nature of time. A traditional realist position in ontology is that time and space have existence apart from the human mind. Idealists, including Kant, claim that space and time are mental constructs used to organize perceptions, or are otherwise surreal.

Suppose that one is sitting at a table, with an apple in front of him or her; the apple exists in space and in time, but what does this statement indicate? Could it be said, for example, that space is like an invisible three-dimensional grid in which the apple is positioned? Suppose the apple, and all physical objects in the universe, were removed from existence entirely. Would space as an "invisible grid" still exist? René Descartes and Leibniz believed it would not, arguing that without physical objects, "space" would be meaningless because space is the framework upon which we understand how physical objects are related to each other. Newton, on the other hand, argued for an absolute "container" space.

The pendulum swung back to relational space with Einstein and Ernst Mach. While the absolute/relative debate, and the realism debate are equally applicable to time and space, time presents some special problems of its own. The *flow* of time has been denied in ancient times by Parmenides and more recently by J. M. E. McTaggart in his paper *The Unreality of Time*. The *direction* of time, also known as "time's arrow", is also a puzzle, although physics is now driving the debate rather than philosophy.

It appears that fundamental laws are time-reversible and the arrow of time must be an "emergent" phenomenon, perhaps explained by a statistical understanding of thermodynamic entropy. Common-sense tells us that objects *persist* across time, that there is some sense in which you are the same person you were yesterday, in which the oak is the same as the acorn, in which you perhaps even can step into the same river twice.

Philosophers have developed two rival theories for how this happens, called "endurantism" and "perdurantism". Broadly speaking, endurantists hold that a whole object exists at each moment of its history, and the same object exists at each moment. Perdurantists believe that objects are four-dimensional entities made up of a series of temporal parts like the frames of a movie.

An Analytical Study

Notably, a number of individuals have suggested that metaphysics as a whole should be rejected. David Hume argued with his empiricist principle that all knowledge involves either relations of ideas or matters of fact:

> If we take in our hand any volume; of divinity or school metaphysics, for instance; let us ask, *Does it contain any abstract reasoning concerning quantity or number?* No. *Does it contain any experimental reasoning concerning matter of fact and existence?* No. Commit it then to the flames: for it can contain nothing but sophistry and illusion.
>
> — David Hume

However, Hume's assertion may be self-defeating if it itself is not self-evident or empirically verifiable. Proceeding from Kant's statement about antinomy, A.J. Ayer in "Language, Truth and Logic" using the verifiability theory of meaning concluded that metaphysical propositions were neither true nor false but strictly meaningless, as were religious views. However, Karl Popper argued that metaphysical statements are not *meaningless* statements, but rather not *fallible*, *testable* or *provable* statements i.e.

neither empirical observations nor logical arguments could falsify metaphysical statements to show them to be true or false. Hence, a metaphysical statement usually implies an *idea* about the world or about the universe, which may be reasonable but is ultimately not empirically testable.

Remarkably, Rudolf Carnap, in his book *Philosophy and Logical Syntax,* used the concept of verifiability to reject metaphysics.

> Metaphysicians cannot avoid making their statements nonverifiable, because if they made them verifiable, the decision about the truth or falsehood of their doctrines would depend upon experience and therefore belong to the region of empirical science. This consequence they wish to avoid, because they pretend to teach knowledge which is of a higher level than that of empirical science. Thus they are compelled to cut all connection between their statements and experience; and precisely by this procedure they deprive them of any sense.

Now we turn to metaphysical poetry.

METAPHYSICAL POETRY

After having a thorough analysis of Mysticism, in this chapter we will introduce you to metaphysical poetry.

It is significant to note that the metaphysical poets were a loose group of British lyric poets of the 17th century, who shared an interest in metaphysical concerns and a common way of investigating them, and whose work was characterised by inventiveness of metaphor (these involved comparisons being known as metaphysical conceits). These poets were not formally affiliated; most of them did not even know or read each other. Their poetry was influenced greatly by the changing times, new sciences and the new found debauched scene of the 17th century.

In *Life of Cowley* (from Samuel Johnson's 1781 work of biography and criticism *Lives of the Most Eminent English Poets*), Johnson refers to the beginning of the seventeenth century in which there "appeared a race of writers that may be termed the metaphysical poets". This does not necessarily imply that he intended metaphysical to be used in its true sense, in that he was probably referring to a witticism of John Dryden, who said of John Donne: "He affects the metaphysics, not only in his satires, but in his amorous verses, where nature only should reign; and perplexes the minds of the fair sex with nice speculations of philosophy, when he should engage their hearts, and entertain them with the softnesses of love. In this . . . Mr. Cowley has copied him to a fault." Probably the only writer before Dryden to speak of a certain metaphysical school or group of metaphysical poets is Drummond of Hawthornden (1585–1649), who in one of his letters speaks of "metaphysical Ideas and Scholastical Quiddities."

Salient Features

Their style was characterized by wit and metaphysical conceits—far-fetched or unusual similes or metaphors, such as in Andrew Marvell's comparison of the soul with a drop of dew; in an expanded epigram format, with the use of simple verse forms, octosyllabic couplets, quatrains or stanzas in which length of line and rhyme scheme enforce the sense. The specific definition of wit which Johnson applied to the school was: "*...a kind of* discordia concours*; a combination of dissimilar images,* or discovery of occult resemblances in things apparently unlike." Their poetry diverged from the style of their times, containing neither images of nature nor allusions to classical mythology, as were common. Several metaphysical poets, especially John Donne, were influenced by Neo-Platonism. One of the primary Platonic concepts found in metaphysical poetry is the idea that the perfection of beauty in the beloved acted as a remembrance of perfect beauty in the eternal realm. In a famous definition Georg Lukács, the Hungarian Marxist critic, described the school's common trait of "looking beyond the palpable" and "attempting to erase one's own image from the mirror in front so that it should reflect the *not-now* and *not-here*" as foreshadowing existentialism. Though secular subjects drew them (in particular matter drawn from the new science, from the expanding geographical horizons of the period, and from dialectic) there was also a strong casuistic element to their work, defining their relationship with God. .

An Anlysis

Critical opinion of the school has been varied. Johnson claimed that "they were not successful in representing or moving the affections" and that neither "was the sublime more within their reach." Generally, his criticism of the poets' style was grounded in his assertion that "Great thoughts are always general," and that the metaphysical poets were too particular in their search for novelty. He did concede, however, that "they...sometimes stuck out unexpected truth" and that their work is often intellectually, if not emotionally stimulating. The group was to have a significant influence on 20th-century poetry, especially through T.S. Eliot, whose favourable essay *The Metaphysical Poets* (1921) helped bring their poetry back into favor with readers.

Main Literary Figures

- John Donne (1572–1631)
- George Herbert (1593–1633)
- Andrew Marvell (1621–1678)
- Saint Robert Southwell (c. 1561–1595)
- Richard Crashaw (c. 1613–1649),
- Thomas Traherne (1636 or 1637 – 1674)
- Henry Vaughan (1622–1695)
- George Chapman (c. 1559–1634)
- Thomas Carew (1595–1640)
- Abraham Cowley (1618–1667),

- Edward Herbert (1583–1648)
- Richard Leigh
- Katherine Philips (1632–1664),
- Sir John Suckling (1609–1642)
- Edward Taylor (c. 1642–1729)
- Anne Bradstreet (c. 1612–1672)
- John Wilmot, 2nd Earl of Rochester (1647–1680)

REFERENCES

Butchvarov, Panayot (1979). *Being Qua Being: A Theory of Identity, Existence and Predication*. Bloomington and London: Indiana University Press.

Gale, Richard M. (2002). *The Blackwell Guide to Metaphysics*. Oxford: Blackwell.

Harris, E. E. (1965). *The Foundations of Metaphysics in Science*. London: George Allen and Unwin.

Kant, I (1781). *Critique of Pure Reason*.

Kim, J. and Ernest Sosa Ed. (1999). *Metaphysics: An Anthology*. Blackwell Philosophy Anthologies.

Le Poidevin R. & al. Ed. (2009). *The Routledge Companion to Metaphysics*. New York, Routledge.

Loux, M. J. (2006). *Metaphysics: A Contemporary Introduction* (3rd ed.). London: Routledge.

Lowe, E. J. (2002). *A Survey of Metaphysics*. Oxford: Oxford University Press.

11
John Donne

A noted and representative write of metaphysical movement is John Donne. Here in this chapter we will introduce you to the learned poet, his poetry and metaphysical/mystic elements in his works.

John Donne was an English poet, preacher and a major representative of the metaphysical poets of the period. His works are notable for their realistic and sensual style and include sonnets, love poetry, religious poems, Latin translations, epigrams, elegies, songs, satires and sermons.

His poetry is noted for its vibrancy of language and inventiveness of metaphor, especially as compared to that of his contemporaries. Despite his great education and poetic talents, he lived in poverty for several years, relying heavily on wealthy friends. In 1615 he became an Anglican priest and, in 1621, was appointed the Dean of St Paul's Cathedral in London.

John Donne was born on Jan. 21, 1572 in London, England, into a Roman Catholic family at a time when open practice of that religion was illegal in England. Donne was the third of six children. His father, also named John Donne, was of Welsh descent, and a warden of the Ironmongers Company in the City of London. Donne's father was a respected Catholic who avoided unwelcome government attention out of fear of being persecuted for his religious faith. Donne's father died in 1576, leaving his wife, Elizabeth Heywood, the responsibility of raising their children. Elizabeth Heywood was also from a recusant Catholic family, the daughter of John Heywood, the playwright, and sister of Rev. Jasper Heywood, a Jesuit priest and translator. She was a great-niece of the Catholic martyr Thomas More. This tradition of martyrdom would continue among Donne's closer relatives, many of whom were executed or exiled for religious reasons.

Donne was educated privately; however there is no evidence to support the popular claim that he was taught by Jesuits. Donne's mother married Dr. John Syminges, a wealthy widower with three children, a few months after Donne's father died. In 1577, his mother died, followed by two more of his sisters, Mary and Katherine, in 1581. Donne was a student at Hart Hall, now Hertford College, Oxford, from the age of 11. After three years at Oxford he was admitted to the University of Cambridge, where he studied for another three years.He was unable to obtain a degree from either institution because of his Catholicism, since he could not take the Oath of Supremacy required of graduates.

Remarkably, in 1591 he was accepted as a student at the Thavies Inn legal school, one of the Inns of Chancery in London. In 1592 he was admitted to Lincoln's Inn, one of the Inns of Court. His brother Henry was also a university student prior to his arrest in 1593 for harbouring a Catholic priest, William Harrington (priest), whom Henry betrayed under torture.Harrington was drawn and quartered, i.e. tortured on the rack, hanged until not quite dead, then was subjected to disembowelment.Henry Donne died in Newgate prison of bubonic plague, leading John Donne to begin questioning his Catholic faith. During and after his education, Donne spent much of his considerable inheritance on women, literature, pastimes and travel. Although there is no record detailing precisely where he traveled, it is known that he traveled across Europe and later fought with the Earl of Essex and Sir Walter Raleigh against the

Spanish at Cádiz (1596) and the Azores (1597) and witnessed the loss of the Spanish flagship, the *San Felipe*. According to Izaak Walton, who wrote a biography of Donne in 1640:

> "... he returned not back into England till he had stayed some years, first in Italy, and then in Spain, where he made many useful observations of those countries, their laws and manner of government, and returned perfect in their languages."

By the age of 25 he was well prepared for the diplomatic career he appeared to be seeking. He was appointed chief secretary to the Lord Keeper of the Great Seal, Sir Thomas Egerton, and was established at Egerton's London home, York House, Strand close to the Palace of Whitehall, then the most influential social centre in England.

During the next four years he fell in love with Egerton's niece Anne More, and they were married just before Christmas in 1601 against the wishes of both Egerton and her father, George More, Lieutenant of the Tower. This ruined his career and earned him a short stay in Fleet Prison, along with the priest who married them and the man who acted as a witness to the wedding. Donne was released when the marriage was proven valid, and soon secured the release of the other two. Walton tells us that when he wrote to his wife to tell her about losing his post, he wrote after his name: *John Donne, Anne Donne, Un-done.*

It was not until 1609 that Donne was reconciled with his father-in-law and received his wife's dowry. Following his release, Donne had to accept a retired country life in Pyrford, Surrey. Over the next few years he scraped a meagre living as a lawyer, depending on his wife's cousin Sir Francis Wolly to house him, his wife, and their children. Since Anne Donne had a baby almost every year, this was a very generous gesture.

Though he practiced law and worked as an assistant pamphleteer to Thomas Morton, he was in a constant state of financial insecurity, with a growing family to provide for. Anne bore him 12 children in 16 years of marriage (including two stillbirths—their eighth and then in 1617 their last child); indeed, she spent most of her married life either pregnant or nursing. The 10 surviving children were named Constance, John, George, Francis, Lucy (after Donne's patroness Lucy, Countess of Bedford, her godmother), Bridget, Mary, Nicholas, Margaret and Elizabeth. Francis, Nicholas and Mary died before they were ten. In a state of despair, Donne noted that the death of a child would mean one less mouth to feed, but he could not afford the burial expenses.

During this time Donne wrote, but did not publish, *Biathanatos,* his defence of suicide. His wife died on 15 August 1617, five days after giving birth to their twelfth child, a still-born baby. Donne mourned her deeply, including writing the 17th Holy Sonnet. He never remarried; this was quite unusual for the time, especially as he had a large family to bring up.

Major Works

Poetry

- *Poems* (1634)
- *Poems on Several Occasions* (2001)
- *Love Poems* (1905)
- *John Donne: Divine Poems (includes the Holy Sonnets), Sermons, Devotions and Prayers* (1990)
- *The Complete English Poems* (1991)
- *John Donne's Poetry* (1991)
- *John Donne: The Major Works* (2000)
- *The Complete Poetry and Selected Prose of John Donne* (2001)

Prose

- *Six Sermons* (1633)
- *Fifty Sermons* (1649)
- *Paradoxes, Problemes, Essayes, Characters* (1652)
- *Essayes in Divinity* (1651)

- *Sermons Never Before Published* (1661)
- *John Donne's 1622 Gunpowder Plot Sermon* (1996)
- *Devotions Upon Emergent Occasions and Death's Duel* (1999; first published in 1624)

Critical Works

- John Carey, *John Donne: Life, Mind and Art*, (London 1981)
- A. L. Clements (ed.) *John Donne's Poetry* (New York and London, 1966)
- Stevie Davies, *John Donne* (Northcote House, Plymouth, 1994)
- T. S. Eliot, "The Metaphysical Poets", *Selected Essays*, (London 1969)
- G. Hammond (ed.) The Metaphysical Poets: A Casebook, (London 1986)
- Sir Geoffrey Keynes, *Bibliography of Donne*, (Cambridge, 1958)
- George Klawitter, *The Enigmatic Narrator: The Voicing of Same-Sex Love in the Poetry of John Donne* (Peter Lang, 1994)
- Arthur F. Marotti, *John Donne, Coterie Poet*, (Madison: University of Wisconsin Press, 1986)
- H. L. Meakin, *John Donne's Articulations of the Feminine*, (Oxford, 1999)
- Joe Nutt, *John Donne: The Poems*, (New York and London 1999)
- E.M. Simpson, *A Study of the Prose Works of John Donne*, (Oxford, 1962)
- C. L. Summers and T. L. Pebworth (eds.) *The Eagle and the Dove: Reassessing John Donne* (Columbia: University of Missouri Press, 1986)
- John Stachniewski, *The Persecutory Imagination*, (Oxford, 1991)
- Ceri Sullivan, *The Rhetoric of the Conscience in Donne, Herbert, and Vaughan* (Oxford 2008)
- James Winny, *A Preface to Donne* (New York, 1981)
- Francis William Teodoro, *A New Tomorrow Needs Us*
- James Lyle Canda, *Someone is Needing My Love*
- Pauline T.C Algas, *Two Against My One Heart*

Early Poetry

Donne's earliest poems showed a developed knowledge of English society coupled with sharp criticism of its problems. His satires dealt with common Elizabethan topics, such as corruption in the legal system, mediocre poets, and pompous courtiers. His images of sickness, vomit, manure, and plague assisted in the creation of a strongly satiric world populated by all the fools and knaves of England. His third satire, however, deals with the problem of true religion, a matter of great importance to Donne.

He argued that it was better to examine carefully one's religious convictions than blindly to follow any established tradition, for none would be saved at the Final Judgment, by claiming "A Harry, or a Martin taught [them] this." Donne's early career was also notable for his erotic poetry, especially his elegies, in which he employed unconventional metaphors, such as a flea biting two lovers being compared to sex. In *Elegy XIX: To His Mistress Going to Bed*, he poetically undressed his mistress and compared the act of fondling to the exploration of America. In *Elegy XVIII*, he compared the gap between his lover's breasts (the intermammary sulcus) to the Hellespont.

Donne did not publish these poems, although did allow them to circulate widely in manuscript form. Donne was elected as Member of Parliament for the constituency of Brackley in 1602, but this was not a paid position and Donne struggled to provide for his family, relying heavily upon rich friends. The fashion for coterie poetry of the period gave him a means to seek patronage and many of his poems were written for wealthy friends or patrons, especially Sir Robert Drury, who came to be Donne's chief patron in 1610. Donne wrote the two *Anniversaries*, *An Anatomy of the World* (1611) and *Of the Progress of the Soul*, (1612), for Drury.

While historians are not certain as to the precise reasons for which Donne left the Catholic Church, he was certainly in communication with the King, James I of England, and in 1610 and 1611 he wrote two anti-Catholic polemics: *Pseudo-Martyr* and *Ignatius his Conclave*. Although James was pleased with Donne's work, he refused to reinstate him at court and instead urged him to take holy orders. At length, Donne acceded to the King's wishes and in 1615 was ordained into the Church of England. Donne became a Royal Chaplain in late 1615, Reader of Divinity at Lincoln's Inn in 1616, and received a Doctor of Divinity degree from Cambridge University in 1618. Later in 1618 he became chaplain to Viscount Doncaster, who was on an embassy to the princes of Germany. Donne did not return to England until 1620.

In 1621 Donne was made Dean of St Paul's, a leading (and well-paid) position in the Church of England and one he held until his death in 1631. During his period as Dean his daughter Lucy died, aged eighteen. It was in late November and early December 1623 that he suffered a nearly fatal illness, thought to be either typhus or a combination of a cold followed by the seven-day relapsing fever. During his convalescence he wrote a series of meditations and prayers on health, pain, and sickness that were published as a book in 1624 under the title of *Devotions upon Emergent Occasions*. later became well known for its phrase "for whom the bell tolls" and the statement that "no man is an island". In 1624 he became vicar of St Dunstan-in-the-West, and 1625 a Royal Chaplain to Charles I.

He earned a reputation as an eloquent preacher and 160 of his sermons have survived, including the famous Death's Duel sermon delivered at the Palace of Whitehall before King Charles I in February 1631.

Later Poetry

It is pertinent to note that some have speculated that Donne's numerous illnesses, financial strain, and the deaths of his friends all contributed to the development of a more somber and pious tone in his later poems. The change can be clearly seen in "An Anatomy of the World" (1611), a poem that Donne wrote in memory of Elizabeth Drury, daughter of his patron, Sir Robert Drury. This poem treats Elizabeth's demise with extreme gloominess, using it as a symbol for the Fall of Man and the destruction of the universe. The poem "A Nocturnal upon S. Lucy's Day, Being the Shortest Day", concerns the poet's despair at the death of a loved one. In it Donne expresses a feeling of utter negation and hopelessness, saying that "I am every dead thing...re-begot / Of absence, darkness, death."

This famous work was probably written in 1627 when both Donne's friend Lucy, Countess of Bedford, and his daughter Lucy Donne died. Three years later, in 1630, Donne wrote his will on Saint Lucy's day (13 December), the date the poem describes as "Both the year's, and the day's deep midnight."

In fact, the increasing gloominess of Donne's tone may also be observed in the religious works that he began writing during the same period. His early belief in the value of skepticism now gave way to a firm faith in the traditional teachings of the Bible. Having converted to the Anglican Church, Donne focused his literary career on religious literature. He quickly became noted for his sermons and religious poems. The lines of these sermons would come to influence future works of English literature, such as Ernest Hemingway's *For Whom the Bell Tolls*, which took its title from a passage in Meditation XVII of Devotions upon Emergent Occasions, and Thomas Merton's *No Man is an Island*, which took its title from the same source. Towards the end of his life Donne wrote works that challenged death, and the fear that it inspired in many men, on the grounds of his belief that those who die are sent to Heaven to live eternally. One example of this challenge is his Holy Sonnet X, from which come the famous lines "Death, be not proud, though some have called thee / Mighty and dreadful, for thou art not so." Even as he lay dying during Lent in 1631, he rose from his sickbed and delivered the Death's

Duel sermon, which was later described as his own funeral sermon. Death's Duel portrays life as a steady descent to suffering and death, yet sees hope in salvation and immortality through an embrace of God, Christ and the Resurrection

It is thought that his final illness was stomach cancer, although this has not been proved. He died on 31 March 1631 having written many poems, most only in manuscript. Donne is buried in St Paul's Cathedral, where a memorial statue of him was erected with a Latin epigraph probably composed by himself.

Literary Style

It is significant to note that John Donne was famous for his metaphysical poetry in the 17th century. His work suggests a healthy appetite for life and its pleasures, while also expressing deep emotion. He did this through the use of conceits, wit and intellect—as seen in the poems "The Sun Rising" and "Batter My Heart". Donne is considered a master of the metaphysical conceit, an extended metaphor that combines two vastly different ideas into a single idea, often using imagery. An example of this is his equation of lovers with saints in "The Canonization".

Unlike the conceits found in other Elizabethan poetry, most notably Petrarchan conceits, which formed clichéd comparisons between more closely related objects (such as a rose and love), metaphysical conceits go to a greater depth in comparing two completely unlike objects, although sometimes in the mode of Shakespeare's radical paradoxes and imploded contraries. One of the most famous of Donne's conceits is found in "A Valediction: Forbidding Mourning" where he compares two lovers who are separated to the two legs of a compass. Donne's works are also witty, employing paradoxes, puns, and subtle yet remarkable analogies. His pieces are often ironic and cynical, especially regarding love and human motives.

Common subjects of Donne's poems are love (especially in his early life), death (especially after his wife's death), and religion. John Donne's poetry represented a shift from classical forms to more personal poetry. Donne is noted for his poetic metre, which was structured with changing and jagged rhythms that closely resemble casual speech (it was for this that the more classical-minded Ben Jonson commented that "Donne, for not keeping of accent, deserved hanging"). Some scholars believe that Donne's literary works reflect thc changing trends of his life, with love poetry and satires from his youth and religious sermons during his later years.

Other scholars, such as Helen Gardner, question the validity of this dating—most of his poems were published posthumously (1633). The exception to these is his *Anniversaries* which were published in 1612 and *Devotions upon Emergent Occasions* published in 1624. His sermons are also dated, sometimes specifically by date and year. His work has received much criticism over the years, especially concerning his metaphysical form.

Donne's immediate successors in poetry tended to regard his works with ambivalence, while the Neoclassical poets regarded his conceits as abuse of the metaphor. He was revived by Romantic poets such as Coleridge and Browning, though his more recent revival in the early twentieth century by poets such as T. S. Eliot tended to portray him as an anti-Romantic.

Donne in Literature

Donne has appeared in several works of literature:

- A dying John Donne scholar is the main character of Margaret Edson's Pulitzer prize-winning play *Wit* (1999), which was made into the film *Wit* starring Emma Thompson.
- Donne's *Songs and Sonnets* feature in *The Calligrapher* (2003), a novel by Edward Docx.

- In the 2006 novel, The Meaning of Night by Michael Cox, Donne's works are frequently quoted.
- John Donne appears, along with his wife Ann and daughter Pegge, in the award-winning novel *Conceit* (2007) by Mary Novik.
- Joseph Brodsky has a poem called "Elegy for John Donne".
- The love story of John Donne and Ann More is the subject of Maeve Haran's 2010 historical novel, "The Lady and the Poet."

REFERENCES

David Colclough, 'Donne, John (1572–1631)', Oxford Dictionary of National Biography, Oxford University Press, September 2004; online edn, October 2007 [2] accessed 18 May 2010

Donne, John in Venn, J. & J. A., *Alumni Cantabrigienses*, Cambridge University Press, 10 vols, 1922–1958.

Greenblatt, Stephen. *The Norton anthology of English literature*, Eighth edition. W. W. Norton and Company, 2006.

Jokinen, Anniina. "The Life of John Donne." Luminarium. 22 June 2006. Accessed 22 January 2007.

Lapham, Lewis. *The End of the World.* Thomas Dunne Books: New York, 1997. p. 98.

Le Comte, Edward. *Grace to a Witty Sinner: A Life of Donne*, (Walker, 1965)

Lim, Kit. *John Donne: An Eternity of Song*, Penguin, 2005.

Stubbs, John. *Donne: The Reformed Soul*, Viking, 2006.

Warnke, Frank J. *John Donne*, (U of Mass., Amherst 1987)}}

12
Conclusion

The discussion made in the preceding chapters have put ample light on mysticism and metaphysics in literature. We have discussed all salient features, trends and other characteristics in detail.

Here in this chapter we intend to present the essence of entire theme in nutshell for quick review.

Those who are interested in that special attitude towards the universe which is now loosely called "mystical," find themselves beset by a multitude of persons who are constantly asking—some with real fervour, some with curiosity, and some with disdain—"What *is* mysticism?" When referred to the writings of the mystics themselves, and to other works in which this question appears to be answered, these people reply that such books are wholly incomprehensible to them.

On the other hand, the genuine inquirer will find before long a number of self-appointed apostles who are eager to answer his question in many strange and inconsistent ways, calculated to increase rather than resolve the obscurity of his mind. He will learn that mysticism is a philosophy, an illusion, a kind of religion, a disease; that it means having visions, performing conjuring tricks, leading an idle, dreamy, and selfish life, neglecting one's business, wallowing in vague spiritual emotions, and being "in tune with the infinite." He will discover that it emancipates him from all dogmas—sometimes from all morality—and at the same time that it is very superstitious. One expert tells him that it is simply "Catholic piety," another that Walt Whitman was a typical mystic; a third assures him that all mysticism comes from the East, and supports his statement by an appeal to the mango trick. At the end of a prolonged course of lectures, sermons, tea-parties, and talks with earnest persons, the inquirer is still heard saying—too often in tones of exasperation—"What *is* mysticism?"

I dare not pretend to solve a problem which has provided so much good hunting in the past. It is indeed the object of this little essay to persuade the practical man to the one satisfactory course: that of discovering the answer for himself. Yet perhaps it will give confidence if I confess pears to cover all the ground; or at least, all that part of the ground which is worth covering. It will hardly stretch to the mango trick; but it finds room at once for the visionaries and the philosophers, for Walt Whitman and the saints.

Here is the definition:—

> *Mysticism is the art of union with Reality. The mystic is a person who has attained that union in greater or less degree; or who aims at and believes in such attainment.*

It is not expected that the inquirer will find great comfort in this sentence when first it meets his eye. The ultimate question, "What is Reality?"—a question, perhaps, which never occurred to him before—is already forming in his mind; and he knows that it will cause him infinite-distress. Only a mystic can answer it: and he, in terms which other mystics alone will understand. Therefore, for the time being, the practical man may put it on one side. All that he is asked to consider now is this: that the word "union" represents not so much a rare and unimaginable operation, as something which he is doing, in a vague, imperfect fashion, at every moment of his conscious life; and doing with intensity and thoroughness in all the more valid moments of that life. We know a thing only by uniting with it; by assimilating it; by an interpenetration of it and ourselves. It gives itself to us, just in so far as we give ourselves to it; and it is because our outflow towards things is usually so perfunctory and so languid, that our comprehension of things is so perfunctory and languid too. The great Sufi who said that "Pilgrimage to the place of the wise, is to escape the flame of separation" spoke the literal truth. Wisdom is the fruit of communion; ignorance the inevitable portion of those who "keep themselves to themselves," and stand apart, judging, analysing the things which they have never truly known.

Because he has surrendered himself to it, "united" with it, the patriot knows his country, the artist knows the subject of his art, the lover his beloved, the saint his God, in a manner which is inconceivable as well as unattainable by the looker-on. Real knowledge, since it always implies an intuitive sympathy more or less intense, is far more accurately suggested by the symbols of touch and taste than by those of hearing and sight. True, analytic thought follows swiftly upon the contact, the apprehension, the union: and we, in our muddle-headed way, have persuaded ourselves that this is the essential part of knowledge—that it is, in fact, more important to cook the hare than to catch it. But when we get rid of this illusion and go back to the more primitive activities through which our mental kitchen gets its supplies, we see that the distinction between mystic and non-mystic is not merely that between the rationalist and the dreamer, between intellect and intuition. The question which divides them is really this: What, out of the mass of material offered to it, shall consciousness seize upon—with what aspects of the universe shall it "unite"?

It is notorious that the operations of the average human consciousness unite the self, not with things as they really are, but with images, notions, aspects of things. The verb "to be," which he uses so lightly, does not truly apply to any of the objects amongst which the practical man supposes himself to dwell. For him the hare of Reality is always ready-jugged: he conceives not the living lovely, wild, swift-moving creature which has been sacrificed in order that he may be fed on the deplorable dish which he calls "things as they really are." So complete, indeed, is the separation of his consciousness from the facts of being, that he feels no sense of loss. He is happy enough "understanding," garnishing, assimilating the carcass from which the principle of life and growth has been ejected, and whereof only the most digestible portions have been retained. He is not "mystical."

But sometimes it is suggested to him that his knowledge is not quite so thorough as he supposed. Philosophers in particular have a way of pointing out its clumsy and superficial character; of demonstrating the fact that he habitually mistakes his own private sensations for qualities inherent in the mysterious objects of the external world. From those few qualities of colour, size, texture, and the rest, which his mind has been able to register and classify, he makes a label which registers the sum of his own experiences. This he knows, with this he "unites"; for it is his own creature. It is neat, flat, unchanging, with edges well defined: a thing one can trust. He forgets the existence of other conscious creatures, provided with their own standards of reality. Yet the sea as the fish feels it, the borage as the bee sees it, the intricate sounds of the hedgerow as heard by the rabbit, the impact of light on the eager face of the primrose, the landscape as known in its vastness to the wood-louse and ant—all these experiences, denied to him for ever, have just as much claim to the attribute of Being as his own partial and subjective interpretations of things.

Because mystery is horrible to us, we have agreed for the most part to live in a world of labels; to make of them the current coin of experience, and ignore their merely symbolic character, the infinite gradation of values which they misrepresent. We simply do not attempt to unite with Reality. But now and then that symbolic character is suddenly brought home to us. Some great emotion, some devastating visitation of beauty, love, or pain, lifts us to another level of consciousness; and we are aware for a moment of the difference between the neat collection of discrete objects and experiences which we call the world, and the height, the depth, the breadth of that living, growing, changing Fact, of which thought, life, and energy are parts, and in which we "live and move and have our being." Then we realise that our whole life is enmeshed in great and living forces; terrible because unknown. Even the power which lurks in every coal-scuttle, shines in the electric lamp, pants in the motor-omnibus, declares itself in the ineffable wonders of reproduction and growth, is supersensual. We do but perceive its results.

The more sacred plane of life and energy which seems to be manifested in the forces we call "spiritual" and "emotional"—in love, anguish, ecstasy, adoration—is hidden from us too. Symptoms, appearances, are all that our intellects can discern: sudden irresistible inroads from it, all that our hearts can apprehend. The material for an intenser life, a wider, sharper consciousness, a more profound understanding of our own existence, lies at our gates. But we are separated from it, we cannot assimilate it; except in abnormal moments, we hardly know that it is. We now begin to attach at least a fragmentary meaning to the statement that "mysticism is the art of union with Reality." We see that the claim of such a poet as Whitman to be a mystic lies in the fact that he has achieved a passionate communion with deeper levels of life than those with which we usually deal—has thrust past the current notion to the Fact: that the claim of such a saint as Teresa is bound up with her declaration that she has achieved union with the Divine Essence itself. The visionary is a mystic when his vision mediates to him an actuality beyond the reach of the senses. The philosopher is a mystic when he passes beyond thought to the pure apprehension of truth. The active man is a mystic when he knows his actions to be a part of a greater activity. Blake, Plotinus, Joan of Arc, and John of the Cross—there is a link which binds all these together: but if he is to make use of it, the inquirer must find that link for himself. All four exhibit different forms of the working of the contemplative consciousness; a faculty which is proper to all men, though few take the trouble to develop it. Their attention to life has changed its character, sharpened its focus: and as a result they see, some a wider landscape, some a more brilliant, more significant, more detailed world than that which is apparent to the less educated, less observant vision of common sense. The old story of Eyes and No-Eyes is really the story of the mystical and unmystical types. "No-Eyes" has fixed his attention on the fact that he is obliged to take a walk. For him the chief factor of existence is his own movement along the road; a movement which he intends to accomplish as efficiently and comfortably as he can. He asks not to know what may be on either side of the hedges. He ignores the caress of the wind until it threatens to remove his hat. He trudges along, steadily, diligently; avoiding the muddy pools, but oblivious of the light which they reflect.

"Eyes" takes the walk too: and for him it is a perpetual revelation of beauty and wonder. The sunlight inebriates him, the winds delight him, the very effort of the journey is a joy. Magic presences throng the roadside, or cry salutations to him from the hidden fields. The rich world through which he moves lies in the fore-ground of his consciousness; and it gives up new secrets to him at every step. "No-Eyes," when told of his adventures, usually refuses to believe that both have gone by the same road. He fancies that his companion has been floating about in the air, or beset by agreeable hallucinations.

We shall never persuade him to the contrary unless we persuade him to look for himself. Therefore it is to a practical mysticism that the practical man is here invited: to a training of his latent faculties, a bracing and brightening of his languid consciousness, an emancipation from the fetters of appearance, a turning of his attention to new levels of the world. Thus he may become aware of the universe which the spiritual artist is always trying to disclose to the race. This amount of mystical perception—this "ordinary contemplation," as the specialists call it—is possible to all men: without it, they are not wholly conscious, nor wholly alive. It is a natural human activity, no more involving the great powers and sublime experiences of the mystical saints and philosophers than the ordinary enjoyment of music involves the special creative powers of the great musician. As the beautiful does not exist for the artist and poet alone—though these can find in it more poignant depths of meaning than other men—so the world of Reality exists for all; and all may participate in it, unite with it, according to their measure and to the strength and purity of their desire. "For heaven ghostly," says *The Cloud of Unknowing*, "is as nigh down as up, and up as down; behind as before, before as behind, on one side as other.

Inasmuch, that whoso had a true desire for to be at heaven, then that same time he were in heaven ghostly. For the high and the next way thither is run by desires, and not by paces of feet."

None therefore is condemned, save by his own pride, sloth, or perversity, to the horrors of that which Blake called "single vision"—perpetual and undivided attention to the continuous cinematograph performance, which the mind has conspired with the senses to interpose between ourselves and the living world.

After having a thorough and meticulous revision of the discussion contained in this volume may have enlightened you to know the theme. To conclude, it may be safely surmised that mysticism and metaphysics are not the themes of a particular epoch of literary history but these are of eternal worth. Modern and coming generations of literary figures will cherish it and adopt in their writings.

Bibliography

Adams, Ansel. *America's Wilderness: the Photographs of Ansel Adams, with the Writings of John Muir*, Philadelphia, PA: Courage Books, 2002

Anderson, William. *The Scottish Nation: Or. The Surnames, Families, Literature, Honours, and Biographical History of the People of Scotland*. London: A. Fullarton Co., 1877.

Bowman, Mary Ann. *Western mysticism: A guide to the basic works*.

Butchvarov, Panayot (1979). *Being Qua Being: A Theory of Identity, Existence and Predication*. Bloomington and London: Indiana University Press.

Carmody, Denise L. & John T. Carmody. *Mysticism: Holiness east and west*. Oxford: Oxford University Press, 1996.

Colby, William (December, 1967). "The Story of the Sierra Club". *Sierra Club Bulletin*. Sierra Club.

David Colclough, 'Donne, John (1572–1631)', Oxford Dictionary of National Biography, Oxford University Press, September 2004; online edn, October 2007 [2] accessed 18 May 2010

Donne, John in Venn, J. & J. A., *Alumni Cantabrigienses*, Cambridge University Press, 10 vols, 1922–1958.

Ehrlich, Gretel. *John Muir: Nature's Visionary*. Washington, D.C.: National Geographic Society, 2000.

Fleck, Richard F. (February 1978). "John Muir's Evolving Attitudes toward Native American Cultures". *American*

Indian Quarterly (University of Nebraska Press) 4 (1): 19–31.

Fox, Stephen R. (1985). *The American conservation movement : John Muir and his legacy*. Univ of Wisconsin Press. p. 30.

Gale, Richard M. (2002). *The Blackwell Guide to Metaphysics*. Oxford: Blackwell.

Greenblatt, Stephen. *The Norton anthology of English literature*, Eighth edition. W. W. Norton and Company, 2006.

Happold, F.C. *Mysticism: A study and an anthology*. London, England: Penguin, 1963.

Harris, E. E. (1965). *The Foundations of Metaphysics in Science*. London: George Allen and Unwin.

Holmes, Steven. *The Young John Muir: An Environmental Biography*. Madison: Univ. of Wisconsin Press, 1999. p. 178.

Horne, *James. Beyond Mysticism* (1978). The moral mystic (1983).

Huegel, F. von. *The mystical element of religion*. 2 vols., London: Dent, 1908; New York: Dutton, 1923.

John Muir (1917). "The Cruise of the Corwin". Boston and New York: Houghton Mifflin Company.

Jokinen, Anniina. "The Life of John Donne." Luminarium. 22 June 2006. Accessed 22 January 2007.

Kant, I (1781). *Critique of Pure Reason*.

Katz, Steven, ed. *Mysticism and language* (1992). London and New York: Oxford University Press.

Katz, Steven, ed. *Mysticism and philosophical analysis* (1978). London and New York: Oxford University Press.

Katz, Steven, ed. *Mysticism and religious traditions* (1983). London and New York: Oxford University Press.

Kim, J. and Ernest Sosa Ed. (1999). *Metaphysics: An Anthology*. Blackwell Philosophy Anthologies.

Lapham, Lewis. *The End of the World.* Thomas Dunne Books: New York, 1997 p. 98.

Le Comte, Edward. *Grace to a Witty Sinner: A Life of Donne*, (Walker, 1965)

Le Poidevin R. & al. Ed. (2009). *The Routledge Companion to Metaphysics*. New York, Routledge.

Lim, Kit. *John Donne: An Eternity of Song*, Penguin, 2005.

Loux, M. J. (2006). *Metaphysics: A Contemporary Introduction* (3rd ed.). London: Routledge.

Lowe, E. J. (2002). *A Survey of Metaphysics*. Oxford: Oxford University Press.

Marquis, Amy Leinbach. (Fall 2007.) "A Mountain Calling", *National Parks Magazine*, retrieved on 23 October 2009.

McGinn, Bernard. *The foundations of mysticism.* New York: Crossroad Press, 1991.

Miller, Barbara Kiely. *John Muir*, Gareth Stevens Publ. (2008) p. 10

Muir, John and Teale, Edwin Way. *The Wilderness World of John Muir*, Mariner Books (1954, 2001)

Otto, Rudolf. *The idea of the holy.* London: Oxford University Press, 1958.

Scholem, Gershom. *Kabbalah*. New York: Dorset Books, 1974.

Scholem, Gershom. *Major trends in Jewish mysticism*. New York: Schocken Books, 1961. (First published in 1941.)

Scholem, Gershom. *Major trends in Jewish mysticism*. New York: Schocken Books, 1961. (First published in 1941.)

Spurgeon, Caroline F E. Mysticism and English Literature. Cambridge University Press. Cambridge, 1913.

Staal, Frits. *Exploring mysticism*. London, England: Penguin, 1975.

Stace, W. T. *Mysticism and philosophy*. Philadelphia: J. B. Lippencott, 1960.

Stubbs, John. *Donne: The Reformed Soul*, Viking, 2006.

Thompson, Francis. Selected Poems Burns and Oates. London, 1908

Underhill, Evelyn. *Mysticism*, 12th edition. New York: Meridian Books, 1955.

Underhill, Evelyn. *Practical Mysticism*. New York: E. P. Dutton, 1915.

Warnke, Frank J. *John Donne*, (U of Mass., Amherst 1987)}}

Weeks, Andrew. *German mysticism. Albany*, New York: SUNY Press, 1993.

Wenk, Elizabeth, and Kathy Morey. *John Muir Trail: The Essential Guide to Hiking America's Most Famous Trail*. Berkeley, CA: Wilderness Press, 2007.

Wolfe, Linnie Marsh, *Son of the Wilderness: The Life of John Muir*, Alfred A. Knopf, 1945.

Woods, Richard, ed. *Understanding Mysticism*. New York: Image Books, 1980.

Wordsworth, William, *A Choice of Wordsworth's Verse*. Selected with an Introduction by R S Thomas. Faber and Faber. London, 1971

Zaehner, R.C. *Mysticism: Sacred and Profane*. London: Oxford, 1961.

Glossary

Absurdism: Philosophy stating that the efforts of man to find meaning in the universe will ultimately fail because no such meaning exists (at least in relation to man). Absurdism is related to existentialism, though should not be confused with it, nor nihilism.

Altruism: The belief that people have a moral obligation to serve others or the "greater good"; term coined by Auguste Comte. Generally opposed to *self-interest* or *egoism*.

Anarcho-syndicalism: A form of anarchism which allies itself with syndicalism, that is, with labor unions, as a force for revolutionary social change. Anarcho-syndicalists seek to replace capitalism and the state with a democratically worker-managed means of production. They seek to abolish the wage system and most forms of private property.

Antinomianism: In theology is the idea that members of a particular religious group are under no obligation to obey the laws of ethics or morality as presented by religious authorities. Antinomianism is the polar opposite of legalism, the notion that obedience to a code of religious law is necessary for salvation. The term has become a point of contention among opposed religious authorities. Few groups or sects explicitly call themselves "antinomian", but the charge is often levelled by some sects against competing sects.

Arminianism: A school of soteriological thought in Protestant Christian theology founded by the Dutch theologian

Jacobus Arminius. Arminianism is closely related to Calvinism (or Reformed theology), and the two systems share both history and many doctrines in common.

Asceticism: Denotes a life which is characterised by refraining from worldly pleasures (austerity). Those who practice ascetic lifestyles often perceive their practices as virtuous and pursue them to achieve greater spirituality. In a more cynical context, ascetic may connote some form of self-mortification, ritual punishment of the body or harsh renunciation of pleasure. However the word certainly does not necessarily imply a negative connotation.

Careerism: The desire to advance one's own career as a sole aim in life, often at the expense of personal and social growth or development.

Colbertism: A variation of mercantilism, which has applied in France between 1661 and 1683 by the superintendent of Finances Jean-Baptiste Colbert.

Comtism: Auguste Comte's positivistic philosophy that metaphysics and theology should be replaced by a hierarchy of sciences from mathematics at the base to sociology at the top.

Conceptualism: A doctrine in philosophy intermediate between nominalism and realism, that universals exist only within the mind and have no external or substantial reality.

Consequentialism: The belief that what ultimately matters in evaluating actions or policies of action are the consequences that result from choosing one action or policy rather than the alternative.

Constructivism: The view that reality, or at least our knowledge of it, is a value-laden subjective construction rather than a passive acquisition of objective features.

Darwinism: A pejorative term for the scientific theory of evolution used mostly by its opponents. This theory was first presented by Charles Darwin in his 1859 book *The Origin of Species*. It stated that the variety of life found on Earth is due to the process of evolution driven by the mechanism of natural selection. It is to be contrasted with Creationism and Intelligent Design. There is a lively debate as to whether or not the theory of evolution is compatible with any, all or some religions.

Emanationism: Belief that reality necessarily proceeds from a first Principle.

Emotionalism: An inclination to rely on or place too much value on emotion. It could be argued that very few, if any, people would label themselves "emotionalists", but rather that it would be a derogatory term applied to them, possibly for exhibiting a zealous demeanor, which may be interpreted as an appeal to emotion.

Empiricism: The doctrine that all knowledge ultimately comes from experience, denying the notion of innate ideas or *a priori* knowledge about the world. It is opposed with rationalism.

Eudaimonism: A system of ethics that evaluates actions in terms of their capacity to produce happiness.

Expressionism: An aesthetic and artistic movement that distorted reality for enhanced or overexaggerated emotional effect. It can also apply to some literature; the works of Franz Kafka and Georg Kaiser are often said to be expressionistic, for example.

Falsificationism: The idea that a proposition or theory cannot be scientific if it does not admit the possibility of being shown to be false. For example, the proposition "All crows are black" is a scientific proposition because it can be falsified by the observation of one white crow.

Finalism: The philosophy that any event is defined by an already-set final outcome and that all events leading up to that outcome are shaped the end result.

Gnosticism: Various mystical initiatory religions, sects and knowledge schools, which were most prominent in the first few centuries CE. It is also applied to modern revivals of these groups and, sometimes, by analogy to all religious movements based on secret knowledge gnosis, thus can lead to confusion.

Hegelianism: A philosophy developed by Georg Wilhelm Friedrich Hegel which can be summed up by a favorite motto by Hegel "The rational alone is real". Which means that all reality is capable of being expressed in rational categories. His goal was to reduce to a more synthetic unity the system of transcendental idealism.

Illusionism: A philosophy that holds that there is no material world but rather a collection of illusions formed by human consciousness that results in an environment for all humans to live in.

Immaterialism: A philosophy that holds that there are no material objects, but rather all reality is a construct of a flawed perception.

Immoralism: The philosophy that man should try to strive for the perfect aesthetic of eternal life.

Immortalism: Another name for immortality (or eternal life), is the concept of existing for a potentially infinite, or indeterminate length, of time. Throughout history, humans have had the desire to live forever. What form an unending or indefinitely-long human life would take, or whether it is even possible, has been the subject of much speculation, fantasy, and debate.

Inductionism: The scientific philosophy where laws are "induced" from sets of data. As an example, one might measure the strength of electrical forces at varying distances from charges and induce the inverse square law of electrostatics.

Intentionalism: A philosophy that questions the underpinnings of original intent and explores whether or not humans are the source of their own actions or are controlled by a higher power.

Interactionism: A philosophy that explores the relationship between cause and effect in regards to the human perception of the universe.

Internalism: In epistemology, the view that all evidence involved in justification must be knowable to the subject.

Irrationalism: A philosophy which claims that science is inferior to intuition, with art and the conquest of the aesthetic being the ultimate transcendence of the humanity.

Meliorism: The idea in metaphysics that humans can, through their interference with natural processes, produce an improvement over the natural outcome. It is at the foundation of contemporary liberal democracy and human rights, and is contrasted by the concept apologism.

Mysticism: The pursuit of achieving communion, identity with, or conscious awareness of ultimate reality, the divinity, spiritual truth, or God through direct experience, intuition, or insight. Traditions may include a belief in the literal existence of dimensional realities beyond empirical perception, or a belief that a *true* human perception of the world goes beyond current logical reasoning or intellectual comprehension.

Necessitarianism: A metaphysical principle that denies that any facts or events are contingent or indeterminate, from human actions to the laws of physics themselves.

Nihilism: Philosophical view that the world, and especially human existence, is without meaning, purpose, comprehensible truth, or essential value. It is more often a charge leveled against a particular idea than a position to which someone is overtly subscribed. Movements such as Dada, Deconstructionism, and punk have been described by various observers as "nihilist".

Nontheism: The absence of belief in both the existence *and* non-existence of a deity (or deities, or other numinous phenomena). The word is often employed as a blanket term for all belief systems that are not theistic, including atheism (both strong and weak) and agnosticism, as well as certain Eastern religions like Confucianism, Taoism, and Zen Buddhism.

Operationalism: The philosophy of defining a concept as the operations that will measure the concept (variables) through specific observations.

Pacifism: In ethics or politics, an opposition to war or violence. Can range from advocacy of peaceful solutions to problems, to a stance where all violence or force is considered morally wrong.

Pandeism: Combines deism (above) with pantheism (under theism, below) to propose a deistic God that becomes a pantheistic Universe; coined by Moritz Lazarus and Heymann Steinthal in *Zeitschrift für Völkerpsychologie und Sprachwissenschaft* (1859).

Perfectionism: A philosophy which holds that the persistence of will should be used in obtaining the optimal quality of spiritual, mental, physical, and material being.

Personalism: School of thought that consists of three main principles: 1) only people are real (in the ontological sense), 2) only people have value, and 3) only people have free will. Personalism flourished in the early 20th century at Boston University in a movement known as Boston Personalism and led by theologian Borden Parker Bowne.

Phenomenalism: In epistemology and the philosophy of perception, *phenomenalism* is the view that physical objects do not exist as things in themselves but only as perceptual phenomena or sensory stimuli (e.g. redness, hardness, softness, sweetness, etc.) situated in time and in space. In particular, phenomenalism reduces talk about physical objects in the external world to talk about *bundles of sense-data*.

Polytheism: Belief in, or worship of, multiple gods or

divinities. Most ancient religions were polytheistic, holding to pantheons of traditional deities, often accumulated over centuries of cultural interchange and experience. The belief in many gods does not contradict or preclude also believing in an all-powerful all-knowing supreme being.

Pragmatism: Philosophy which originated in the United States in the late 19th century. Pragmatism is characterized by the insistence on consequences, utility and practicality as vital components of meaning and truth. Pragmatism objects to the view that human concepts and intellect represent reality, and therefore stands in opposition to both formalist and rationalist schools of philosophy. Rather, pragmatism holds that it is only in the struggle of intelligent organisms with the surrounding environment that theories acquire significance, and only with a theory's success in this struggle that it *becomes* true.

Quasi-realism: A non-cognitivist, expressivist meta-ethical and epistemological theory developed by professor Simon Blackburn. It holds that although propositions supervene on states of mind, they have many realist characteristics, such as only being able to change slowly or in response to changes in natural properties.

Randianism: The individualist movement founded by Ayn Rand, known by its adherents as objectivism.

Reconstructivism: A philosophy which holds that societies should continually reform in order to establish a more perfect government or social network.

Reliabilism: In epistemology, the claim that the status of a belief as *knowledge* should be judged by whether it was arrived upon through a reliable method. For instance, scientific experiment may be considered a more reliable method than intuition or guesswork.

Representationalism: A philosophical concept that states that we do not (and can not) perceive the external world directly; instead we know only our ideas or interpretations of objects in the world. Thus, a barrier or a veil of perception prevents first-hand knowledge of anything beyond it. The "veil" exists between the mind and the existing world.

Romanticism: A philosophy that expresses art as an emotional experience based on the appreciation of the aesthetic. In other words, Romanticism is a philosophy where art is celebrated due to the emotional reaction on the part of the receiver.

Scientism: The belief that science has primacy over other ways of obtaining knowledge. This term is often used in a derogatory manner, to refer to a level of trust or reliance upon scientific progress which the speaker deems excessive.

Scotism: The philosophical school and theological system named after John Duns Scotus. It heavily criticized the Old Franciscan School and thomism.

Secularism: In politics, the notion of the independence of the state from religion; the advocacy of a state which is neutral on matters of religious belief. Secularism, or religious freedom, is usually considered to go both ways: the state should not compel the people to follow (or not follow) a religion; and likewise religious doctrines should not control the actions of the state.

yncretism: The attempt to reconcile disparate, even opposing, beliefs and to meld practices of various schools of thought. It is especially associated with the attempt to merge and analogize several originally *discrete* traditions, especially in the theology and mythology of religion, and thus assert an underlying unity.

Teleologism: The supposition that there is design, purpose, directive principle, or finality in the works and processes of nature, and the philosophical study of that purpose. Teleology stands in contrast to philosophical naturalism, and both ask questions separate from the questions of science. While science investigates natural laws and phenomena, Philosophical naturalism and teleology investigate the existence or non-existence of an organizing principle behind those natural laws and phenomena. Philosophical naturalism asserts that there are no such principles. Teleology asserts that there are.

Theological noncognitivism: The argument that religious language, and specifically words like "God" (capitalized), are not cognitively meaningful. It is cited as proof of the nonexistence of anything named "God", and therefore is a basis for atheism. There are two main arguments: Kai Nielsen used verifiability theory of meaning to conclude that religious language is meaningless because it is not verifiable, proving weak atheism. George H. Smith used an attribute-based approach to argue that the concept "god" has no meaningful attributes, only negatively defined or relational attributes, making it meaningless — leading to the conclusion that "god does not exist", thus proving strong atheism.

Thomism: The philosophical school that followed in the legacy of Thomas Aquinas. The word comes from the name of its originator, whose summary work *Summa Theologiae* has arguably been second to only the Bible in importance to the Catholic Church.

Utilitarianism: Theory of ethics based on quantitative maximization of total welfare for a specific population of humans. It is a form of consequentialism. Welfare is generally described hedonistically. Utilitarianism is summarized as "The greatest happiness for the greatest number."

Utopianism: The many various social and political movements, and a significant body of religious and secular literature, based upon the idea that paradise is achievable on earth.

Index

T

U

W

Y

Z

■■■